POETRY now

POETIC TALES

Edited by

Becki Mee

First published in Great Britain in 1999 by
POETRY NOW
1-2 Wainman Road, Woodston,
Peterborough, PE2 7BU
Telephone (01733) 230746
Fax (01733) 230751

All Rights Reserved

Copyright Contributors 1998

HB ISBN 0 75430 560 0
SB ISBN 0 75430 561 9

FOREWORD

Although we are a nation of poetry writers we are accused of not reading poetry and not buying poetry books: after many years of listening to the incessant gripes of poetry publishers, I can only assume that the books they publish, in general, are books that most people do not want to read.

Poetry should not be obscure, introverted, and as cryptic as a crossword puzzle: it is the poet's duty to reach out and embrace the world.

The world owes the poet nothing and we should not be expected to dig and delve into a rambling discourse searching for some inner meaning.

The reason we write poetry (and almost all of us do) is because we want to communicate: an ideal; an idea; or a specific feeling. Poetry is as essential in communication, as a letter; a radio; a telephone, and the main criteria for selecting the poems in this anthology is very simple: they communicate.

CONTENTS

The Awkward Customer	Colin Skilton	1
Recession - England (1990)	Sioux	2
A Lovers' Tiff	Christopher Irwin Poynter	3
A Wet November Sunday	I Maclaren	4
The West End Cafe	Elisabeth Walters	5
Remember . . .	Lannette Lusk	6
The Churchyard Murder	Sheila Taunton	7
A Voyage Into Eternity	Nigel Astell	8
Duel	Jill Barker	9
The Handyman	Donato Genchi	10
Forever Young	Diana Meek	10
The Ambulance Service	Dennis N Davies	11
Heaven And Hell	MacGregor Holmes	12
Bullfight	Ian Brittle	12
The Helpless Ones	Mary Cotter	13
The Visitor	A Bayes	14
There But For The Grace	Trisha Williams	15
Dead Poets Watch Quietly	Sue Knight	16
Down Moon To Nirvana	Brian J Rapier	17
Elysian Fields	Maureen Atkin	18
Aspects Of Apartheid	William L I Newman	19
The Haunted House	R L Cooper	20
When She's Thin!	J L Thorne	21
Foetus	G C Dymock	22
A Place Of Rest	Shelley Williams	22
The Goodbye Man	Jeremy Bell	23
Prince Of Darkness	Rachael Shipston	24
Encounter On A Country Lane	Ian C Gray	25
A Special Place	Joyce West	26
Not Astronomically Likely!	John Morris	27
Romeo And Juliet	U Johnson	28
From A Child, To A Child, For A Child	M J P Durbidge	28
Requiem For A Village	M Ward Hunt	29
The Saga Of The WI Visit To Hampton Court	Jennie Rippon	30

'Ni Sa Bula' - Hello And Welcome	Susan Holmquist	31
Bliss	Glenn R Lumb	32
Holiday Romance	A P Stevens	33
Old English	Alec G Wright	34
'Star[R]' (Report 1998)	Barbara Sherlow	35
Full Circle	Nigel Hunt	36
The Morning After	Roger Williams	37
The Frog	Brenda Barker	38
The Countryside Rally	Penny Rendle	39
Twilight Journey	W B McDade	40
Desecration	C Baudains	40
In Memory	Margaret Trimby	41
For A Sad Poet	Richard Flemington	42
Killer	Elizabeth Mark	43
Forty Six - One- Fifty One	Pat Heppel	44
Poor Me	Ursula Pinner	45
Gone Forever	Danielle Pinner	46
Cader Idris	John Remmington	47
Mind Frustrating	S A Hawkshaw	48
Picard's Fish	Jason J Rorbach	49
An Episode In The Life Of Gerry The Gerbil	Judy Eldridge	50
Screen Icon - Robert Mitchum	Pat Foster	51
Wired/Wings	Aka Jazz	52
Charles Dickens	Valerie Marshall	53
A Forgotten Man	Paul Anthony Kearsey	54
Winter Friends	Joyce Shipton	55
Juliet's Lament	M Deuchars	56
Engaging Thoughts	Alison Jane Lewcock	56
The Bystander	Rita Smith	57
Every Poem	Peggy Dugdale	58
Through The Mists Of Time	Anne James	58
Ashtray	Lefort	59
The Thames Tramp	Carole Murphy	60
My Perfect Day	Joan Mayer	61
Receptionists In Waiting Rooms	John Jeffrey Howie	62
The Diamond Jubilee	Ann Saxty	63

Alone	Cath Spooner	64
Broken Spirit	Pamela Buxton	65
A Lover's Lament	V R Broster	66
7, All Saints' Passage, Cambridge	Elizabeth Moberly	66
The Wedding	Norma Thorpe	67
Salad Days	P Knowles	68
Famine	F England	68
Burning Bush Symphony	Olga Allen	69
My Life	Paul Chapman	70
Layman's Opinion	Tricia Nolan	71
This Is Our Time	Trevor F Woollacott	72
Autumn	Phyllis Gage	73
Abandoned	Andrea Smith	74
National Lottery	Bill Bright	75
Untitled	Joyce Humphrey	76
Robbing The Kestrel's Nest	H D Hensman	77
Life's Destiny	Phoebe J Laing	78
How Do I Answer?	Jo Rosson Gaskin	79
Dracula's Bride	Kirstie Clark	80
Death Of An Orange-Picker	Martin Clarke	81
Why Is It?	Olive Wright	82
Standing In The Need Of Prayer	Deborah Davis	82
Billy Moore	John Hewins	83
The Granite Mariner	Frank Schofield	84
Nightmare	Sidney Headley	85
Health Is Wealth	Stephanie Bowler	86
The Artist Versus Nature	Dorothea Payn Le Sueur	87
Desperandum - Help!	Joanna Pickett	88
Emergence	Terry Harnwell	89
Growing Old Together	Roger Plowden	90
Holiday Blues	Chris Saunders	91
I Wish I Could Have Known You	Keren Newth	92
I'm Glad We Met	Paula E Jones	93
Untitled	E Hollihead	94
Payback Story	Thomas P Brown	94
Nightmare	Barnaby Newman	95

Don't Look At My Clothes, Look At Me	Katina Hilliard Sharpe	96
Death	Lez Walsworth	97
Road To Recovery	J L M	98
We All Fell Down The Stairs	Sean Brown	99
The Remains Of Each Day	Trevor Vincent	100
To All The Anna Karenias Of The World	Tahira	101
Never Too Late	M J Prebble	102
The Elopement Of Lady Betty Charteris	Dennis Tackley	103
Home Village	Joan Smith	104
Ode To Temping	Sally Thompson	105
A Lost Journey	Fred Schofield	106
Unwelcome Guest	Audrey Bate	107
Joel 2 V 25 . . .	A Langley	108
My Garden	Margaret Nuttall	109
Autumn	John A McHale	110
Be Like A Lion	Sue Chadwick	110
The Letter On The Mat	P R McDonald	111
Boiling Point	Mark Dobbs	112
That Sinking Feeling	Ray Baker	113
The Catch	Susan Davis	114
The Painting	Henry J Green	115
Exist	Gary Ridley	116
An Occasional Reminder	Debbie Gibson	117
A Love Unfolds	Margaret Webb & Irene Leese	118
One Glass Eye	Annie Lovelock	120
March 13th	Jill Bramham	121
Vision	Stephen Keyes	122
My Baby	Dorothy Aplin	122
Teardrop	Denis Catley	123
A Synopsis Of The Weather	M C Lawrence	124
Day And Night	Karen Bethell	125
A War Zone	Valerie Barton	126
Whirlpool	Tracey Wheeler	127
Every Poem	Andrew Walker	128
When Tribal Man Returned	Coleen O'Brien	129

The Ballad Of Fun	Helen Steel	130
Homeward Bound	Jessica M A Thomas	131
My Little Kite	R Widd	132
The Journey Home	Barry Busby	133
The Net	M E C Houlden	134
Back To Work	Yvonne Neal	135
Stand And Stare	Eileen St John-Crees	136
The Chasuble Of Saint Ildefonso	John C Stratton	137
Greater Love	H Collister	138
Overheard On The Highway	Barbara Tunstall	139
Goldfish Recycling	Meinir	140
The Tramp	Cynthia C Berry	141
Natural Laws	Eric Ashwell	142
Stones Upon The Water	David C Love	143
Harry's Willow	Frances Whitaker	144
The Confession	Jeanette Dykes	145
Child Missing	Gwen Place	146
King Of The Cue	Kopan Mahadeva	147
Northern Inter-Reality	Simon Dale Leeman	148
The Place	W H Lunn	149
Tale Of The Century	David Price Edwards	150
Final Call	Clive W Macdonald	151
When First We Met	Hazel Barber	152
A Long-Lost Moment	Saleha Chowdhury	153

THE AWKWARD CUSTOMER

Right said Les, let's look at the airplane
see if the rivets are in the right place
oh dear blighty not very likely
they're getting nowhere
and so we brought another three

So right said Les let's look at the motor
see if the engine's in the right cc
oh dear crikey not very likely
this engine's going nowhere
and so we brought another three

So right said Les let's have a butchers
see if the panel pins are in the right place
oh cor blimey not very likely
these pins are holding nowhere
and so we brought another three

It occurs to me as likely
if they ask me or invite me
to tell them what to see
they could be as good as me

So right said Les let's look at the model
see if the propellers are in the right place
oh dear rightly not very likely
this airplane's going nowhere
and so

Simon and me hit him with a big fee
and then we went home.

Colin Skilton

RECESSION - ENGLAND (1990)

It's raining, it's pouring, it's freezing cold
It's windy, it's grey, it's a miserable day.

No work, no money, nothing to do
There's a deep feeling of blue.

No smiling, no laughing, nothing to say
Enthusiasm rates darker than grey.

Depression, unhappiness - utter despair
Bitterness and resentment choke the air.

False promises for *their* personal gain
The politicians play a consequential game.

The banks are just as much to blame
Devastating action - there's no shame.

A numbered puppet on a string
Manipulated under Big Brother's wing.

No one listens - no one cares
The computer's blamed - it bleeps and stares!

The wealthy powered by wanton greed
Don't care how much the country's in need.

The nation divided by social class
Pressures to conform or be outcast.

It's odd that when *things* go wrong
Friends don't give support for long.

There's little hope - no understanding
You're on your own - have a safe landing!

For struggle as you may or might
You'll soon be broken by your fight.

And when you've fallen right down low
The system won't let you grow.

And when *they've* taken all away
It's only left to you to pray.

Sioux

A LOVERS' TIFF

The little cat's feet were twitching
As she sat on back of chair rest
Across the room a candle flickered
Casting shadows across the pine table it rested on
Wine bottles empty stood by glasses the same
Plates empty with knives and forks peacefully resting
Their place was put after meal was eaten
The fruit basket near where bananas climbed oranges
A fire burns in room through arch adjoining
Conversation once in full flow, now silent
Like the vase of flowers gently smiling
In corner of the other room above a family photograph
What was said and is not now somehow cannot be
For who knows what lurks within the shadows unseen
The cat sits now her head hung low 'tween her paws
Now ask me more than this my heart is happy
It's no more than I journeyed or could wish for
Well who knows what the centre of a circle
And who knows where the corners are
Now dimmed the lights and fire extinguished
Creep I silently to my bed in hope tomorrow will I see
Her smile again and us to happy be.
(She did)

Christopher Irwin Poynter

A Wet November Sunday

As now November closes in,
his manner dipped, deep in sin,
      an' raging skies
Trees are stripped, tossed, forlorn,
An age of madness, it seems is born,
      now autumn dies.

My collar up, wrapped round the neck,
upon the bridge, or quarter deck,
      is what it seems,
as driving rain, forced now to pause,
an hour late, a losing cause,
      wade pavement streams.

Cars go whirring through the day,
Anointing huddled folk wi' spray,
      add insults now,
And still the angry heavens weep,
all o'er mankind the torrents sweep,
      like rivers flow.

Football voices flood the park,
youth will always make its mark,
      earthly ties,
no fear of life's inclement storms,
no fear of winter's angry forms,
      or rolling skies:

I Maclaren

THE WEST END CAFE

A warm place to be
On a freezing cold day
I strongly suggest
The West End Cafe

There you will always find
The coming and going
Of young men and women,
And a waiter who's all knowing
If you stay there a while, then
The coffee just keeps flowing

I warn you though
You may find the waiter
Chatting away to two girls
And still there a while later

If they mention 'Whispers'
Then the laughter will roar
As this seems a topic
Which they always want more
But watch out, or the
Young man may be on the floor

If you want to meet people
It's a great place to go
As there you will find all sorts
Who are interested to know
New and different people other
Than those who go with the flow

A warm place to be
On a freezing cold day
I strongly suggest
The West End Cafe.

Elisabeth Walters

Remember...

We clung together, you and I
As we had to stifle a silent cry
Our eyes misted in the still of the night
Waiting, waiting until we saw the light

We'd listen for the step on the stair
I'd hold you and stroke your hair
Our mother's sobs we heard her cry
Knowing, knowing the reason why

In the morning our bodies would ache
The tiredness we suffered of being awake
Our mother's pretty face black and blue
Yes we knew what he had put her through

Oh what he put all of us through!
Not knowing what he may do!
He never hit us but Mother so meek
He thought he was strong but he was so weak

We kept the secret just you and me
Oh how we wanted Mother to be free
She'd wince at the pain he hurt her so much
Her bruises and cuts we could not bear to touch

We'd sit at the table and he'd open the gate
Our breath we would hold if he came in late
The stench of the ale as he came through the door
We'd seen it all so many times before

So I would grasp your little hand tightly
And watch your tiny mouth quiver slightly
With sunken eyes our mother would see
Welcoming the day we could be free

Protecting you my little sister all that I could
Remember, remembering, all that I would
He's long dead now but memories remain
A part of our lives without all the pain

Lannette Lusk

THE CHURCHYARD MURDER

Ghostly shadows cast by the yew trees,
Leaves rustling gently, blown by the breeze.
The night is still - one senses doom,
Evil lurks behind every tomb.

Upon its hinges, the kissing gate,
Swings and groans - awaiting fate.
Suddenly - on this eerie night
The moon breaks through, shining her light.

A flash of silver in hand held high -
From the shadows a feeble cry,
Now a sinister bloodcurdling scream,
Just for a moment - see the knife gleam.

A shrouded shadow appears - and flees,
Melting in shadows cast by the trees.
The silvery moon again hidden by clouds,
Darkness o'er all, spread like a shroud.

The pitiful bundle lies so still -
In the dark - in the churchyard - on the hill.

Sheila Taunton

A Voyage Into Eternity

Dust gathers on the cover,
Pages all yellow with age,
This book of records of long ago,
Shows a date of 1798.
It tells of a shipwreck,
All hands lost on that day,
No mercy shown,
From a fury of an ocean upturned.
Bodies tossed into the waves,
Just as bait thrown to the sinister deep,
All were lost and drowned.
After this fierce storm, washed upon the shore,
The remains of a full sailing vessel,
This wooden frame smashed and battered on the rocks,
Sails torn to shreds, nothing is left.
On a dark misty night, under a full moon,
A silhouette gliding on the horizon can be seen,
Out of the shadows, every 50 years it appears,
An eerie sight of forgotten souls,
Plot a course to pass through an unmarked grave.
Red eyes glare out of the mist,
Staring into motionless space,
A white figure of the captain stood so still,
Hands grasped firmly on the steering wheel,
Strange sounds from ghosts of sailors,
Loud wailing and screaming,
Echo across quiet waters,
Sending ripples of coldness,
A feeling of below zero, to a break of hot sweat.
This is indeed a force from the other side.

Unsettled spirits sailing on and on,
A voyage into eternity,
Will this ghost ship never sink,
And peace found for all inside,
Can the past not be buried,
And laid to rest.
I fear another 50 years must pass,
Before the truth is revealed,
Can this poor imprisoned crew,
Be saved at all,
From an inescapable fate,
All we can do . . . is wait.

Nigel Astell

DUEL

They met at dawn:
Amidst the mist that early autumn morn,
When silence reigned.
Where nothing would be gained:
A clash of blades of steel,
A deadly wound, that never would time heal.
A life so young, what waste,
Because he dared to taste
Those sweets beyond his reach.
Although his love he did beseech
Alas, she to her husband ran,
A wealthy, suave, skilled gentleman.
Who, with the tip as deadly as a dart,
Thrust forth his sword into the young man's heart.

Jill Barker

THE HANDYMAN

I know a bloke that's good with his hands, a handyman,
Sometimes I call him the randy man,
And every time there's DIY to do he takes his tool kit out I've found,
For he's always seen with his screwdriver in his hand -
Always screwing around,
Every time he's happy or sad or on the job, he takes it out,
Whenever he wants to relieve his anger, he takes it out no doubt
When there's a leaking pipe, you know he's got his small spanner out,
He' happiest when he's tightening his nuts and fixing things about
I remember the last time he took his small tool out -
It got caught in the door,
And now his spanner is bent as a banana and he can't use it anymore.

Donato Genchi

FOREVER YOUNG

Can you see past a wrinkle
A head of greying hair
Don't look at me pityingly
As if I am not there
Talk to me a while
Share a word or two
On the outside I am old
Yet on the inside I feel new

Diana Meek

The Ambulance Service

The ambulance service
And paramedic teams.
Emergency
Their siren screams.
In the fast lane
Speed very high.
Blue light flashing
As they, pass by.

A radio call
From their home base.
To an accident
They quickly race.
Skills and technology
Sometimes strained.
But the ambulance crews
Are, highly trained.

In fair weather
Hail rain or snow.
When visibility
Is very very low.
Giving a service
None can compare
There's even an ambulance
In, the air.

Dennis N Davies

HEAVEN AND HELL
(Dedicated to all 'Humanists')

I've never been a believer in life after death, or reincarnation -
I'm sure we've only got this life and its purpose is for creation.
I feel we are all meant to be part of an amazing natural design -
That nature is too perfect a symmetry to be an accident divine,
And what's in the bible is the word of God, spoken through man,
Yet not to be taken literally, but understood as a symbolic plan.

It's nice to believe we should be born into freedom and equality,
But this is an impossible dream in a world that's less than ideal -
All the important issues such as looks, intellect and personality
Are predetermined for us, proving that choice isn't in the deal.
I am converted yet I'm not religious in the church-going sense -
I don't like the Christian idea of Jesus having died for our sins.

As for death, I do not believe that the spirit is going anywhere
And I am sure reward or punishment should be given out here.
We have free will, yet can't always choose our heaven or hell
But the good do find a paradise on earth during their lifetime,
While the bad experience death of the soul before a living hell.
I'd like to believe that for evil there is retribution in our time,
That the great man is all-knowing without actually being here
And that he works through us in a way we have reason to fear.

MacGregor Holmes

BULLFIGHT

Across the arena, swaggering, proud
The bullfighter comes, the roaring crowd
Cheer; walking calmly upon the sand
Waiting there, sword in hand.

Here is the bull! Fearless, menacing
A charge! The fighter dodges, prancing,
Showing his 'courage', under the sun
Then he stabs, and murder is done.

Ian Brittle

THE HELPLESS ONES

The poor dumb creatures of this world, why must they suffer so?
They have a right to peace of mind as much as humans do
Why are they used so cruelly . . . experimented on?
They have no choice but to bear the pain
It's all so very wrong.

The giant creatures of the deep are ruthlessly pursued
And man is never satisfied until the seas run blood.

The fox is chased across the fen by dogs and horses and by men
And animals of every kind in misery are reared in pens.

And fashion's ladies wear their furs and never stop to think
Of all the lives the garments took of beaver, fox and mink.

The tricks the circus creatures do . . . imprisoned lions at the zoo
And little overburdened mokes, and monkeys dressed up in red coats.

'It's my world too' the slogan goes, and that's what God intended
But greedy man has intervened, and nature is up-ended.

When will man stop the exploitation, cease this misery?
Heaven would rejoice a thousand-fold to see all creatures free.

Free to live their natural lives, existence without fear
The present situation palls . . . the cost is far too dear.

Mary Cotter

THE VISITOR

Dave awoke with a startle one night,
his wife lay asleep in the deep of her dream,
he wondered why the room was so bright,
his sleepy eyes, strained at the whitened scene.

Unmoved by his startle, paralysed by the scare,
his wife lay silent, unaware of his fright,
he moved to the window, to see what was there,
out in the garden, this cold winter's night.

The light disappeared as he opened the curtain,
Dave's eyes were adjusting, his heart missed a beat,
the garden looked still, but he almost was certain,
of a figure sat still on the patio seat.

As Dave tried to focus, without being noticed,
he tried to make out, what or who was sat there,
two red blinking eyes, made Dave shrill a cry,
as he looked out again, the eyes disappeared.

His wife, she was troubled by pushing and shoving,
her dream was disturbed by her man at the bed,
instead of the usual, awaken for loving,
sounds of despair had awoke her instead.

By that of great worry and the strength of the story,
the two ventured out holding hands in the dark,
the garden was lit by the rays of the torch,
fear grasped their stomach, like the jaws of a shark.

As they moved to the seat where the eyes had once been,
Dave swerved in half circles, to cover his track,
his wife now shocked by what she had seen,
a note on the seat saying, *'I'll be back.'*

A Bayes

THERE BUT FOR THE GRACE

Just another mugging.
Nothing to do with you.
Just another old lady,
Beaten up black and blue.

Just another rape case.
You heave a judging sigh.
She should have seen it coming,
Short skirt hitched so high.

Just another child snatched.
Step-father disappeared.
Condemn the mother's weakness,
Marrying a man she feared.

Just another headline.
Does your heart feel no tug?
All is well in your neat world,
Safe, secure and snug.

Just another road-rage.
Policeman at your gate.
Drunken youths and your man's dead,
You've lost your life-long mate.

Just another sad tale.
Your world turned upside down.
Pain is indiscriminate,
Compassion - the healing crown.

Trisha Williams

DEAD POETS WATCH QUIETLY

From pauper's grave
By foetid stream,
I flit to groves of academe,
To where Tom Watson, *PhD*.
Expounds upon his subject:
Me.

I've done him proud,
Victorian house
Two lads, a cat,
Adoring spouse,
And in the summer,
Clutching fees,
A class of studious
Japanese.

How strange it is
To watch this man
Explaining how
My verses scan,
See the old settle
Where I sat
Listen bemused,
Did I mean that?

With careless skill
He lists my life,
'This his mistress,
Here his wife,
In these few lines
We think we see
Some homosexuality.'

A cold rage grows
With every word
My children starved,
I died, unheard.
How dares this
Learnéd nonentity
Presume to know one
Such as me?

I raise my hand,
But stay the curse.
Without these,
Who would read
My verse?

Sue Knight

Down Moon To Nirvana

Low and level, in bright moonlight,
bridges skipped rippled water behind,
Target ahead, bomb-doors still tight;
Too low - too close! Oh! Fractured mind.

There go colours of the day
Bomb on the greens soon as they show,
'Select! Bomb Aimer', as I say
vibrating, roaring, round-out! Sky's aglow.

'Course-out Nav? Report damage,'
still alive cold, in panic!
'Steer one-five-zero' I hear - I manage,
she pulls out smoothly; all said - demonic.

Brian J Rapier

Elysian Fields

A cotton-candy froth of clouds
drifts slowly in azure-blue sky
as, bathed in golden sunshine, crowds
amass with floral tributes. I
observe the scene through tear-veiled eyes,
a witness, fraught with disbelief,
engulfed by mourning nation's sighs
and tears shed openly in grief.
Flower-decked verges, clothed in hues
of every shade, grow with each hour
whilst heavenly perfumes interfuse,
potpourried from each scented flower.
Memories spark till thoughts entrance,
though joy and sorrow intertwine,
as flames of lighted candles dance
and flicker mid the petalled shrine.
Caressed by breezes, flowers sway
and paint a Technicolor sea
of waves that take the breath away,
a reverential tapestry.

Our English rose, in perfect bloom,
a Princess taken in her prime,
plucked savagely from Britain's womb,
now lives, eternally, through time.

Maureen Atkin

ASPECTS OF APARTHEID

On the outskirts of town
Where the grass grows tall
There lives a pretty girl
With spring in her eyes
And lips that are warm
And a voice that is soft
With no hint of a frown

On the outskirts of town
Where the sky is blue
There lives a pretty girl
With summer in her smile
And gentle is her touch
And joyful is her laugh
Whenever I call round

On the outskirts of town
Where the air is clear
There lives a pretty girl
With autumn in her hair
And kind are her ways
And truth is her life
And honesty's her crown

On the outskirts of town
Where the river runs free
There lives a pretty girl
With winter in her heart
For although we're in love
We now have to part
Because my skin is coloured brown

William L I Newman

THE HAUNTED HOUSE

We called it the haunted house
Since my dad had called it so.
But whether a house or a factory
We didn't really know.

Past a cemetery and allotments
And an embanked railway line
What it was and whose it was
There wasn't any sign.

One day in a thunderstorm
I took my brambling sisters there.
We sheltered in a doorway
By the well of a rising stair.

Footsteps came from the floor above
And pebbles bounced down the well,
And those stairs were the only way out
As far as we could tell.

Quickly, carefully, quietly,
My intentions not revealing,
I reach the stair top opening,
My eyes ever on the ceiling.

But I found the room quite empty
For the floorboards were all gone.
And of the building's roof tiles
In patches there were none.

'Who was it?' my sisters called.
I could only shake my head.
Nowhere to hide, nowhere to go,
What was there to be said?

Do footsteps disturb the night
Of new houses built on this site?

R L Cooper

WHEN SHE'S THIN!

I have a friend I dearly love, I've known her many years,
we've shared a lot of laughter and our fair share of tears.
She really is quite special but there's one thing that is wrong,
it drives me to distraction and has gone on far too long!

I'll ring her up, 'It's fine today, let's go out for a walk.'
She says 'I'd rather stay indoors, come over for a talk.'
It's not that she hates walking, she just likes being in
and anyway she'll walk each day as soon as she is thin!

So we share another coffee, we laugh, we have a chat,
she shows me her new diet, she says, 'I'm trying that!
I'm starting it tomorrow cause it's too late today
I've made myself hot chocolate and I can't throw it away.'

Now it's not that she's a liar, it's truly her belief
that if she loses 50lbs her life won't cause her grief!
She'll never have an overdraft, she'll never have a fight,
it's obvious if she lost weight her life would be just right!

So every flippin' Monday she starts another fad,
Slimfast, apples, cabbage soup it really drives me *mad!*
By Wednesday she is so fed up she raids the biscuit tin
and shows me clothes she's going to wear . . . as soon as she gets thin!

So we never go out dancing, we don't go for a swim
but soon she'll go she promises . . . as soon as she gets thin!

I wish I could persuade her that life is passing by,
it's not for want of trying and it makes me want to cry.
She's lovely, warm and funny, so what if she's not *'thin'*
I wish she'd take her diet sheets and chuck them in the bin!

J L Thorne

FOETUS

I wasn't planned, I don't know why.
I wasn't meant, yet here am I.
Doubling now and tomorrow,
Growing bigger, to whose sorrow?
It's two months now. I'm alive!
Will I survive?
I'll count my fingers one to ten.
My toes? There's as many of them!
At six months, I'll wriggle and twirl,
Will I be a boy or a cute little girl?
My gender will develop.
My mother I will envelop.
When I've finished growing,
I'll not diminish the owing I have,
For my mum, and my dad!
In this home I wish to huddle.
It's warm, cosy and not in a muddle.
So I'll cuddle and wait,
To see what fate, has bought of me?
I'll see . . .

G C Dymock

A PLACE OF REST

There is a place where I long to be,
A place which is special and meaningful to me.

A gentle silver flowing stream,
Fluffy marshmallow clouds to sleep on and dream.

A silent place where in vacant mood I lie,
A place with no hurt or pain to make me cry.

A place where I will go to and stay,
When the time comes - my dying day.

With pure white angels and cremello fields,
Where protective soldiers stand holding their shields.

And when I weep the pain will flow away,
Like a waterfall falling and running in play.

Shelley Williams

THE GOODBYE MAN

An armchair and a thin, grey man:
A universe of spectral dreams;
He fought the battles of his time
And now sits musing in the streams
Of love and hate and hope and fear,
Of now and when and why and how -
He does not criticise so much
But contemplates the newsprint now -
The weave, the warp, the hidden side,
His life within the maze of thread;
He looks back from the mountaintop,
I see that look - and softly tread
On past him to an empty chair,
Take up my paper - spread my wings
Around the world - the page is bare,
Drum - empty of enduring things!
I glance across - he knows I see
And smiles a last goodbye to me.

Jeremy Bell

Prince Of Darkness

Prince of Darkness, dark eyes flashing, with defiance and hostility.
With a yearning and insatiable hunger.
His reckless lust and erotic bewitching,
Tear all contemptuous chiding asunder.
His stinging kiss and satanic allure,
Provoke her obsessive devotion,
And drown her in the depths of desire.
And there they play their mindless games,
Wildly wanton in their pursuit of the everlasting fire.
He consumes her.
She possesses him -
Their ungovernable passion bleeds them dry.
The ravaging gypsy, tormented by images,
Without his life and soul,
Remorseless, unatoned and inconsolable. He does cry.
And, here I sit on the sidelines, watching this charade,
I pray for some relenting, from this ghostly, demonic parade.
But yet I ponder on the sordid and savage adoration,
And my heart beats ferociously as I gaze upon his face.
My resolution is devoid, usurped by strange elation,
When I imagine myself in his voracious embrace.
I steal another look at the reckless fearsome fiend.
Conceiving the truth of what they all say.
Still, the audacity of my feelings,
Towards the tempestuous tempter astounds me.
As I wish it was I he'd have be with him, always.

Rachael Shipston

ENCOUNTER ON A COUNTRY LANE

'Twas on a dark autumnal day
I saw an old man bent and grey;
With shuffling gait and tapping cane,
He passed along that country lane.

He wore a hat of deepest black,
A great cloak wrapped around his back;
His face was etched with lines of age.
Who was this ancient craggy sage?

His eyes were fixed upon the ground,
He did not see I was around.
Unseeing still he passed by close
This figure in black, with looks morose.

I pitied not this spectre rare.
For age will come to all who share
The passing years of time untold.
What mysteries will time unfold?

This mirror of myself in time;
I turned around, the ghost sublime
Was vanished from that country lane,
But still I heard that tapping cane.

Was this a spectre I had seen,
Or fellow traveller, old and lean?
I now tread on with greater stealth
This figure was my future self.

Ian C Gray

A Special Place

'The old walled garden' - how I love my name
So many years it's been the same,
Huge trees nestle by my side.
Birch, oaks and chestnuts all reside -
'Tis autumn and the leaves now fall
Conkers like missiles
And small boys call; to fill their pockets -
These precious treasures, worth more than any gold could measure -
So freshly varnished a lovely brown
Eighth wonder of the world they've found.
Soon winter now - but not for long -
Wrens, robins and blackbirds will hop along
My old old wall and sing their songs -
Then I shall watch the spring renew,
And paint her picture in the morning dew
In wonderful greens all around my walls -
Then with the warmth of the early sun -
Tiny flowers will slowly come
Sweet roses in the summertime
So many tales that I could tell
Of young and old who walk and dwell
In this special place -
And tho' I'm just an old old wall
I can see and hear the human race
Most times it has a happy face
Like this old old wall

Joyce West

NOT ASTRONOMICALLY LIKELY!

Covent Garden, teeming rain, picture the scene
Near a porticoed church called St Paul's;
Society 'night owls' were casting their spleen
At the cabbies ignoring their calls.

    I gazed at a star with a large, happy throng,
    Some using glasses, two from the Press.
    The distance from us to the star wasn't long -
    A mere twenty feet I would guess!

Our bright evening star was known as Eliza;
She sat in the porch selling flowers.
Prancing through puddles, snobs seemed to despise her,
Whereas I could have watched her for hours.

    'Ow garn' and 'it ain't' in broad Cockney she whined,
    Then was taught how to speak 'la-di-da'.
    But no smart professor - phonetics in mind -
    Could foresee that world-famous faux pas!

Four curtain calls later, I made for the bar;
It was packed, so still feeling beguiled
I went off to catch one more glimpse of the star;
I was lucky! My heart stopped! She smiled!

    She posed with the cast being asked to say 'Che-ee-se'
    Laughing beside a dressing-room door.
    I begged 'Will you give me your autograph, ple-ea-se?'
    She said 'Where have I seen you before?'

'Just a mere stage-door John' she drawled with a grin,
'I'll be glad to get home, husband dear;
And I tell yer aht strite, I'm proper dun in,
So tonight we'll Doolittle I fear!'

John Morris

ROMEO AND JULIET

Across the crowded street,
Their eyes met.
A shaft of blinding light,
In the black night.
The sound of thunder,
They stare in wonder.
In the virginal bed,
She cradles his head.
Caught in her gold hair,
Fusion of dark and fair.
Lost in wonder.
Outside, the crash of thunder.
He is dead. There,
Lying in her hair.
A flash of light,
In the black night.
The unborn baby cries,
As young love dies.

U Johnson

FROM A CHILD, TO A CHILD, FOR A CHILD

Sweet child so peaceful, asleep once more
Unaware of the sickening scenes that abhor
Too young to know all the wrongs and unjust
Not yet awoken to all the troubles and fuss

Snatched moments of heaven, so special, so rare
Don't all of us matter? Don't all of us care?
Intolerance and hatred, causing suffering and pain
Too busy with self and what we can gain

Can we not change? Why can we not see?
That if I had been you, and you had been me
The alternative view to those thoughts we had
Still time for good - from all this bad

Sweet child stay peaceful, asleep no more
Be as one with this world and its beauty adore
With all men and women show love fair and just
Respecting all that this time has placed in your trust

M J P Durbidge

REQUIEM FOR A VILLAGE

Our village is changing,
the old times have gone.
They say it is progress
and time marches on.
Gone are the farmsteads,
the stackyards, and byres,
the warm smell of stables
that housed the big Shires.
No jingle of harness,
no rattling of chains,
now shatter the silence
as they plod up the lanes.
The ring of the anvil,
the village shop's bell,
are now but a memory,
and who could foretell
that houses now stand
where the bullock yards stood,
and children no longer
gather flowers from the wood.

M Ward Hunt

THE SAGA OF THE WI VISIT TO HAMPTON COURT

One Wednesday morn to Hampton Court the WI did go.
The day went really well until we tried to get back home.
The rain came down, the lightning flashed with thunder overhead.
We left the Court at half past five, the sky just looked like lead.
And then we hit a traffic jam to add to our delight.
More often we were stationary although we thought we might
Eventually get moving - what an optimistic lot.
We moved a few yards at a time - thank God it wasn't hot.

And then our driver, Colin, took a left turn off the street
To try to beat the traffic queue - it really was a treat
To feel that we were moving after standing still so long.
We went all through a new estate where the coach did not belong.
We waited for the other coaches which were with our group.
They never came and so we carried on through a new route.
We went round lots of country roads, through Sunbury village too.
We joined another smaller queue but options were so few.

We ended up in Shepperton, not quite the way we came.
But at least we were now moving which was better just the same.
We heard at last the other coach had taken a wrong turn
And had to join the queue again from where it had begun.
We finally found the motorway but it was blocked quite solid,
And when we came to J13 it really was quite horrid.
The exit had been closed because of flooding - what a shame!
And so we carried on along the motorway again.

For a while we hardly moved but slowly it got better.
We almost felt that soon we would have to write a letter
To let the folks at home know that we'd be home quite soon.
At this point I think most of us were desperate for the loo.
We eventually found the services and turned in there to wait
For the others to catch up but it was just their fate
That they were way behind us and we couldn't hang around.
We dived into the loos then went to eat the food we found.

> So it all ended up happily though we were very late.
> It was quarter past eleven as I walked to my gate.
> But we had a really super time - a day I will remember
> And I'd love to go again even though I'm not a member.
> And so I'll put my name down if there's another trip to try.
> And thanks to Colin and of course, thanks to the WI.

> *Jennie Rippon*

'NI SA BULA' - HELLO AND WELCOME

Fiji - hot and steamy, primitive and poor,
We loved you and would always return for more.
People there were friendly, we so enjoyed their ways,
Thinking we'd be bored, we only allowed five days.
We stayed in Hideaway Resort, far from the nearest town,
Our journey there by mini-bus gave us all a chance to look round.
They were building a McDonald's near Nadi
This we were surprised to see,
Then round the corner the sugar cane train rattled on noisily.

From our bure facing the breach,
Palms and mynah birds within easy reach.
We saw exotic flowers, saw coral from a glass-bottomed boat,
Saw a royal blue starfish, learnt to snorkel and float.
We shared in a Fijian wedding,
(where the minister wore a wrap-round skirt)
Drank kava with the village chief, (reached by a track of dirt.)
New Year passed with fireworks, so sorry to leave for home.
Enough memories to fill five notebooks - next year where
                                                         will we roam?

Ask Grandma if she enjoyed the trip and what she liked the best?
'Climbing the extinct volcano - of course I only went for a rest!'
Four islands we had sampled and learnt so much of mankind,
Colour, warmth and beauty, yes, travel certainly broadens the mind.

Susan Holmquist

BLISS

We looked healthy together with our slap-on fake tans,
I'd take you to cafes in my slick Bedford van,
I'd spoil you with snacks from a hot frying pan;
Bacon butty, grease running down your hands.

We popped into a tattooist for a tattoo or two,
He engraved your left breast with a hairy baboon;
A tribute to our love, in a visual, cryptic clue
For you drive me monkey nuts and I'm ape over you.

Having jumped into the sidecar of my oily motor bike,
I vowed you'd stay beside me, never let you out of my sight,
I promised to respect you (never take you for a ride),
Now we've been going out together for a jam-packed,
Fun-filled fortnight.

Saturday night was wrestling night at the Corn Exchange in town,
You'd whistle at the wrestlers as they threw each other around,
At home you'd get to grips with me under the eiderdown,
But how I wish you'd stop that whistling, I feel like a clown.

The studs on your leather jacket suit you to a tee,
Your bright red braces, two-tone laces compliment your jeans,
I know you have teeth missing but it's only dentistry.
That's why I call you 'Molars', my crowned tooth fairy queen.

Stock-car meetings were thrilling, such exhilarating fun,
We watched as cars turned over, left the track and spun,
You squeezed my hand with passion, I knew you were the one,
As we kissed we shared the flavour of your bubble gum.

You were great at making roll-ups, clever with your hands,
Paper planes and daisy chains were always in demand,
You could twist me round your finger like a weakened rubber band,
You've even done a stretch in Holloway, I understand.

I'm glad you're moving in with me, it underlines our faith,
Your pigs and goats can use the lawn as long as we shut the gate,
We could be extremely happy if the neighbours have no complaints,
You and I plus the menagerie on a rowdy council estate.

Glenn R Lumb

HOLIDAY ROMANCE

He was a sad and lonely man
Who'd led a very sheltered life
And so he thought he'd take a trip
To try and find himself a wife.

He went and booked a package deal
With money left from dear old Mum,
And soon he was upon the plane
To topless girls and summer sun!

The small hotel was very nice
Not quite what he had had in mind
No disco bars or swimming pools
Or topless girls that he could find!

The room maid though was very sweet,
She showed him all the local sights,
And so of course, he fell in love
During those long hot days and nights.

So Spain is where you'll find him now
His own hotel beside the sea
He runs it with his sweet young wife,
No more the lonely man is he!

A P Stevens

OLD ENGLISH

Behold I stand in posture grand, lord of all I survey.
Six hundred years I've stood and grown,
The things I've seen and things I've known,
Changing from day to day.
Seasons have come and hurried past,
The wind and storms have taken toll,
But still I stand, my roots hold fast,
My bark is clean like tall ship's mast,
And peace is in my soul.
Sweethearts have come their names to carve,
A lasting signet of their love.
Countless woodmen have gone by,
Their sharpened axes held on high,
I'm spared by God above.
The fauna of the woodland have used me as they will,
For home, for their protection, and to rest.
My canopy of leaves spreads like a roof with eaves,
It's natural accommodation at its best.
Sadly through the passing years,
As if in answer to my fears,
My trunk has become hollow through decay.
This means the end is near, men with chain saws will appear.
And that will be the ending of my day.
But at present I'm supreme, standing proudly in my place.
Facing any weather be it dry or soak.
I'm a symbol, I'm a sign, better than the finest wine.
        I'm a stately, proud and tall, *Old English oak.*

Alec G Wright

'STAR[R]' (REPORT 1998)
(To bring a President down
Starr was/is the 'Star' -
as he evidently intended)

Impeachment - or no?
Turning the political handle
Will the people decide
This Washington scandal.

Do his pleads now fall
On American deaf ears
Will the people survive
And live on Clinton tears.

Throwing himself now on
The vast America mercy
Will the people give way
To President perjury.

However he tries now
Bill cannot escape the badgery
Will the people forgive
And end this tragedy.

Accused of deceit
With shame his head now bows
Will the people ignore
Broken President vows.

Hanging now on a thread
Is he already fired
Will the people return
This man so admired.

Barbara Sherlow

Full Circle

The mother drank; the father swore.
They'd throw him out and shut the door.
. . . He was only four.

He needed love. He cried at night;
They'd lock him in without a light.
. . . Imagine his fright.

He'd back away from human touch;
His little body beaten such
. . . He was bruised so much.

He wet his bed; but no one there
To field the guilt they made him bear
. . . In dread and despair.

And faults they found at every turn.
They threatened him and made him learn
. . . By cigarette burn.

They'd smoke a joint and on a high
Would force the lad to have a try.
. . . He did not dare cry.

At five years old he started school
But soon was breaking every rule.
. . . He thought it was cool.

Withdrawn at play, he shunned a throng;
Was bully to the weaker young.
. . . He had a vile tongue.

But then at last these signs are seen
With dawning light for what they mean;
. . . What he's tried to screen.

His childhood is the very clone
Of what had been his parents' own.
. . . Seed will set as sown.

Nigel Hunt

THE MORNING AFTER

When I woke up this morning,
I'd planned to do some work;
When I got up, my legs collapsed -
Oh, I did feel a berk!

I'd been down to the pub last night,
And had a bottle or two
Of Scotch or rum or some such thing,
Because I had the 'flu.

I must have got back home all right,
And put myself to bed;
But when I woke this morning,
It was . . . Oh, my aching head!

My shirt was lying on the stairs,
My trousers in the bath;
And snoring on the kitchen floor,
I found my girlfriend, Kath.

I'd planned to do some work today,
When I got out of bed;
But, since I didn't have the strength,
I wrote this poem instead!

Roger Williams

THE FROG

My name is Brenda Barker,
I'm a 'Whitehall' MDA.
I look after the kids in the playground,
For an hour and a half each day.

And there's lots of tales that I could tell,
About the school, the kids, the staff,
But, this incident in particular,
Gave us all such a laugh.

In our playground three months ago,
A frog had lost its way,
The 'head' said to find it a new home out the front,
But it was back, the very next day.

Parked in Miss Avery's doorway,
Squashed, and looking dead,
Caused quite a flap, trying to keep the kids back,
She called for the deputy head.

Then Lee, who's done a first aid course,
Looked upon the sight,
And said, I think, he just needs a drink,
And do you know what, she was right.

'Cos when Miss Avery, armed with surgical gloves,
Went to lift his lifeless bod;
Intending to bury him nicely,
Nearly dropped the poor little sod.

When the frog, who wasn't dead at all,
Just feeling 'not quite right',
Tried to make a jump for it,
Gave Miss Avery such a fright.

The kids and us just cracked-up,
I'll never forget that day,
The teacher's face, and the fuss it caused,
The frog that lost its way.

Brenda Barker

THE COUNTRYSIDE RALLY

Thursday Morning dawns bright and clear
Today's the day - July 10th is here.

Coaches are travelling from all corners of the land
the marchers have arrived, don't they look grand
to a demonstration to stop hunting from being banned.

Hyde Park, London - Is the place to be
the countryside people meet for the world to see.
How many thousand would be affected, like me?
We all stand united round the Reformers Tree.

Young and old have come along today
to listen to the speeches and hear what they have to say.
Hunting people from all walks of life
from the Peer of the Realm to the housewife.

They have one thing in common to make Blair understand
what it would mean to the fabric of the land
If he carries out his threat and bans hunting with hounds
shooting will be next on his list - I'll be bound!

Stand up and be counted, march with your feet
show the Labour Party our strength - United they'll never defeat!

Penny Rendle

Twilight Journey

Between daytime and night-time
There comes a time
Vague, shadowy, undefined
And yet for a moment clear
An outline tree stands out against the sky.
Vague shapes loom along the track,
Half-formed and black.
It is the time between night and day,
Time to pause, to rest, to think . . . of what?
For at this time life seems meaningless, unreal,
Yet wait!
Lights bloom out of the gathering gloom,
Signs of hope in a vague world of shadows.
At last the train shudders to a halt,
The end of the world or the beginning?

W B McDade

Desecration

Yesterday the poplar stood proud
And magnificent in full growth maturing green.
Revered survivor of suburban scene
Its splendour sought and claimed the sky,
Gladdened every jaded eye.

Came morning, fellers, truck and saw,
And arrogance to push the law
In the face of sensitivity;
Time denying fair recourse
Desecration took its course.

Nobility so ignominiously deposed,
Eloquent gestures incite a blitz
On centuries of glory. In minutes
Brave heart and sinew mortally exposed
Bleed - slice after tortured amber slice.

This inconvenient remnant of Paradise
Obliterated without redress.
Passing by an old lady measures the emptiness.

C Baudains

In Memory

In a lush green meadow we found you,
Beneath the mountains and a sky so blue.
Amongst your comrades and friends so brave,
Each of you in his solitary grave.
We stood and looked and what we saw
Filled our hearts and minds with awe.
Row upon row of stark white stones.
Beneath which lay our loved ones bones.
We said a prayer and shed our tears,
And thought of all those wasted years.
So young, so brave, you died for us,
Your job you did without much fuss.
Time marches on and people forget,
But we'll be forever in your debt.
To save us all from bitter strife,
You gave your all - You gave your life!

Margaret Trimby

FOR A SAD POET

I see the concealed courage
On your smiling face.
But sense the arid desert
Through which your bruised
Resentful being
Must travel seeking, still,
Those dreams: unborn.

I know the longing that you feel
For life to yield some recompense
For all the work, the effort
With which you've striven
To succeed -
Only to gather: dust!

Let me say this -
I feel for you; and yearn
To make and bring a shining star
To light the silent spaces
Of your lonely mind.

A light -
Whose rays illuminate your soul
With inspiration born anew.
A light guiding you from
That desert of despair,
Towards an oasis, bright,
Of infinite success!

Richard Flemington

KILLER

Today, I turned the corner of my street,
Looked down and saw a chaffinch at my feet,
Lifeless, feathers still a brilliant hue.
I caught my breath, and thought at once of you,
That card you'd sent of small, rich-coloured birds,
Tweeting from fat beaks trite, happy words,
(Banal, but we both loved sub-Disney kitsch.
And often late at night we'd laugh and bitch
About pretentious books, films, plays and art -
And people. God, we'd tear the pseuds apart!)
To shameful verbal depths we would descend.
My wicked, witty, gay and dearest friend.

You said you'd ring me after lunch today.
Your lover rang instead. His voice gave-way.
You'd stepped out on his window ledge this morning.
From four floors up you leapt, crashed through an awning.
He found you on the pavement, broken, dead.
'Please, come and comfort me.' your lover said . . .

Coda

I killed you off in this poem
Because we will never wed.
And I'm jealous as hell of your 'other'
(And Tom, and Chris, and Ed!)

While I was writing this poem
You came home from 'away'
'It's bad luck in spades.
I've got full-blown AIDS.'
The sky turns ashen, grey.
'Come. Take *my* life.' I say . . .

Elizabeth Mark

FORTY SIX - ONE - FIFTY ONE

We lived happily at number 46
For over thirty one years,
When a sudden change of circumstance
Threatened a move I viewed with fear.

Grandma and Grandad had lived at 51,
Their nearness extended the family unit,
Our three children grew up happily,
Only a stone's throw away for a visit!

The years took their toll, illness struck,
My mother was the first to leave us,
Proximity meant I could care for Dad,
Four years later he followed without fuss.

Now strangers moved into 51,
The memories too hard to bear,
With money they had both willed to us,
For our daughter we proposed to care.

Born spastic, she was finding it difficult
To manage the stairs with ease,
Both senior citizens with her to mind
We searched for a bungalow to please.

So many we viewed without success,
Steep hills, too many steps, rooms so small,
Then number 1 - detached, caught our eye,
From those we'd seen, the best one of all!

Yet I worried - were we doing the right thing?
I needed a sign, then I was told,
The new telephone number was 46 1 51,
Our new house number nestled between the two old!

Pat Heppel

Poor Me

Even though you know the truth,
You still cling to all the lies,
Never offered any comfort,
You never heard me cry.
Just shut me out and closed your mind.

It was me who suffered all the pain,
Not you who cried alone,
All I wanted was to be loved,
But you didn't love enough - there was only you.

You only saw your own needs,
Never cared for mine,
For you it was only me, me, me,
You wanted attention all the time,
But now you are on your own,
You still cannot see.

You still do not realise,
The blame you lay with me,
You just closed your mind,
With your eyes you only see,
What you want, never a thought of me.

You just shut me out,
Closed the door and threw away the key,
I bet you are sitting there now - thinking about yourself;
Poor me, poor me, poor me.

Ursula Pinner

GONE FOREVER

In the still summer's evening - I sat waiting.
Counting the minutes as the clock ticked on.
Still waiting, waiting for what!
I did not know.

Later I sat still, still as the quiet summer evening.
Hoping that it wasn't true.
Hoping that in the morning she would still be there.

I cried silently into my hands.
'No, no!' I wanted to shout.
Nan mustn't be dead.
Not Nan, not my Nan!

But the clock ticked on,
And as evening turned to night,
And night to morning,
I knew in my heart it was true.

A week later, maybe even more,
I saw her still and white in her coffin,
With a faint smile etched on her face.

I cried bitter tears,
And tried to hide them behind my hands.
Trying to keep inside the sadness
And the rage that was spilling over.

And I knew then
That Nan was gone forever.

Danielle Pinner (15)

CADER IDRIS

We chose to climb this small mountain
And found a marked out track
We were sure by doing it this way
We could easily find the way back.

It led through a rock strewn gully
So to make a diversion appeared best
And when the climb grew more difficult
We stopped beside a boulder to rest.

The way ahead was rugged and steep
Not easy to keep a grip on the grass
Then, picking our way on loose gravel
When the tufts underfoot became sparse

To have kept to the rock strewn gully
Through which lay the recognised track
Would have avoided our present position
But now there was no turning back.

To move ahead was extremely precarious
To lose footing meant an endless drop down
There was hope on a hill to our left
Where some fencing lay near to it's crown

It was a relief to see those man-made fixings
Linked together with lengths of wire
But before we could grab them for safety
We had to struggle a little bit higher

The fence was on a recognised track
As we followed it's meandering way
We shall never forget those old oak posts
That became the highlight of that day.

John Remmington

MIND FRUSTRATING

Why does my mind keep talking,
Going round in riddles and rhymes,
I could write a story a day
A poem
A play
I could write a book,
On all the thoughts that pass through my mind,
If only
I had the time.

In company I make no conversation,
Just listen and nod on occasion,
But in my head my mind keeps on talking,
Of little
Or no importance.

And sometimes it's just so frustrating,
When I can't speak the sentence,
That's balanced on the end of my tongue,
Then when it escapes,
Shit!
It's wrong.

That's not what I was supposed to say,
It's too late now : Anyway
In my mind is where it will stay,
Going round in riddles and rhymes.

S A Hawkshaw

PICARD'S FISH
(Poem about an adventure on Star Trek : The Next Generation)

The crew of the Enterprise really seemed miffed,
They just flew out of a Tyken's rift,
The bald headed captain sat in his chair,
Worf made a joke that the man had no hair.

Picard faced the Klingon, his cheeks blushed red,
And commented smugly on Worf's cow pat head,
The crew bust out laughing but quickly shut up,
Worf's getting angry, he may kick some butt.

Picard went over to his ready room door,
Which quickly shot open, revealing paw prints on the floor,
The fishtank was still, just an empty space,
A murderous look came across Picard's face.

He picked up his phaser and set it on high,
And thought to himself 'Some cat fur will fly,'
One final look at the fishbowl glass,
Straight off the bridge to blast Spot's little ass.

Computer 'Where is the cat' he does say,
The reply comes sharply 'Spot is in sickbay.'
He enters the room to find Spot on a bed,
With a shot from the Phaser - The moggy was dead.

Wesley turns up to see Spot really tanned,
Silently stunned with Picard's fish in his hand,
You see, he'd taken the fish without Jean-Luc's consent,
All for some daft fish experiment.

Jason J Rorbach

An Episode In The Life Of Gerry The Gerbil

Becky and Danny had Gerry their pet,
They weren't to know gerbils don't like the wet,
Saturday morning they gave him a treat
Aiming to wash from his head to his feet.

Bowl and detergent, plus towel of course,
Water was tepid, just right for his paws,
Deep, so that he could enjoy his first swim,
When all was ready, they popped Gerry in.

Gave him a swirl and squeezed Fairy on top,
Set to with gusto and bubbles and mop.
Claws not for swimming, poor Gerry soon sank,
Steep plastic sides, worse than any fish tank.

Gasping out bubbles, the breast stroke he tried,
Soap gummed his eyes, it was thickly applied.
Coming up helpless he let himself drift,
Tiny and fragile, in need of a lift.

Meanwhile Mum woke and she checked on the kids,
Both rather early up out of their beds.
Going downstairs, heard no sound from the pair,
Wondering, went to look under a chair.

Then saw the bowl and she froze on the spot.
Dread, shock and horror, her stomach a knot.
Called up to Dad who then sped down the stairs,
Took in the facts then looked under the chairs.

Two tear-streaked faces peeked out from the gloom
Waiting for wrath, the pronouncement of doom.
Gerry scooped up, rinsed and tenderly dried,
Warm milk with Brandy pepped up his inside.

Fire on, then massage applied to his chest,
Poor little gerbil, he wanted a rest.
He was now breathing, the kids calming more,
Cuddled together, all sat on the floor.

Gerry got better, his eyesight returned,
Kids growing up, a lesson well learned.

Judy Eldridge

SCREEN ICON - ROBERT MITCHUM

He was a sleepy-eyed hero of the cinema screen,
tall and handsome in a sultry way;
excitingly decadent, I thought at eighteen.

Lazy, laconic, dominating and mean,
stylishly low key and always blasé;
he was a sleepy-eyed hero of the cinema screen.

Back in the forties who would have foreseen
his legendary status, an icon, today;
excitingly decadent, I thought at eighteen.

Trenchcoated, slouching, the ultimate teen dream,
don't let the film ever end, I would pray;
he was a sleepy-eyed hero of the cinema screen.

'Build My Gallows High' I might have seen
or 'Out of the Past' at the matinée;
excitingly decadent, I thought at eighteen.

And now he is dead I'm no longer serene
as I remember lost youth with dismay;
he was a sleepy-eyed hero of the cinema screen,
excitingly decadent, I thought at eighteen.

Pat Foster

WIRED/WINGS

Morning:
Bleak eyes seep silenced words
Broken wings taunt flightless birds
How softly spoken, in jested haste
The blade who enters with fetish taste;
of duck, of chicken, of breast.

Strangers:
Hands which outreach to hold
To be held by anothers muted cold
Of simple screams
and dying dreams;
I wonder aimless in perfection's haze.

Leave:
Sip the ego till the spoon is dry
Splash the tea, make the smudges cry.
Far afield the sun sets golden pearls
In time, close unspoken eyes
To stroke mine beard;
to slowly die.

As you are:
So sullen speech meets with mingled words
And crunching birds grit flightless birds.
Amid an ego that echoes simple screams
and hazy blades to slice bleeding dreams.
Farewell a Princess deep in sleep -
Awake alone
Cuddle your breast;
for it is now yours to keep.

Aka Jazz

CHARLES DICKENS

Dickens was a famous writer,
Whose novels were deep, with a few that were lighter.
Fifteen of those which were of considerable length,
About oddities of human nature and strength,
But most of all displayed a critical eye towards injustice,
And at the same time of comic refulgence.
His childhood he spent painfully in Portsmouth and Chatham,
Then moving to London where his father was imprisoned.
Forced to work in a warehouse he remembered hard conditions,
He later wrote with sympathetic and bitter predictions.
He trained at Court to be a stenographer,
And later he went on to be a reporter.
This gave him a fine eye for many details,
Producing a series of comic sketches for retail.
Nearly all his novels had a social message,
Drawn on personal experience and family passage.
Little Dorrit was a family confined to a debtor's prison,
And Oliver Twist the grim world of the struggle of children;
Hard Times about the cruelty towards the working class,
Whereas Bleak Times attacks the legal system and the top brass.
The best loved and most popular works that he did write,
Was David Copperfield and Great Expectations to many's delight.
He wrote a Christmas Carol; A Tale of Two Cities and Scrooge;
Pickwick Papers; The Old Curiosity Shop and David Copperfield but a few.
His marriage broke up to Catherine Hogarth who had borne his ten children,
Which made him start afresh, reading his works to his brethren.
He lectured twice in America when his life was depleted,
And died before his novel Edwin Drood was completed.
His death after fifty-eight years of hardship and success,
Will go down in history as a novelist at his best.

Valerie Marshall

A Forgotten Man

He sits back in his chair,
Cigarette smoke clutters the air,
Collecting thoughts of those days
Remembering, all his old ways;
When ladies glistened on either arm,
Falling for his boyish charm,
But age has taken away his youth,
All he's left with is, yesterday's truth.

A Royal Command before the King,
Was something that meant everything, to him;
His voice delivered, so strong and clear,
It was the highlight of his career;
For with such style he played the game
His private life came second to the fame,
And still in the light of a cold dark morning,
He can hear an ovation calling.

A sad and lonely man's part is now cast,
That round of applause would be his last,
He waits, with hope, that the telephone may ring,
To someone, somewhere, he may still mean something;
A face cracks in the glaze of time,
A voice diminished as if in mime,
No more encores for him to sustain;
No one left to entertain!

Paul Anthony Kearsey

WINTER FRIENDS

What a rich reward we get
in exchange for a little thought,
It's hard to count the number of birds
that eat the food I bought.

How I wish I could converse
with all my feathered friends,
Or understand what they say to each other
the chatter that never ends.

The noisy Starlings, arguing and shouting
the more refined little Blue Tits,
The Blackbirds and Thrushes just call and leave
content with a very small bit.

The Magpies, aggressive as usual
try to show they are boss,
What a lot of fun I get
By watching all the fuss.

How I shall miss you in summer
when you do not need my food,
But I do know that you will return
to show me your young brood.

Then once again - Winter,
the cold and frosts will be around,
Then you will need my food once more
When the snow is on the ground!

Joyce Shipton

JULIET'S LAMENT

Romeo! Romeo!
Wherefore art thou Romeo?
I need you to kiss me
No matter where or when
To hold my hand
Whether I need it or not
To talk to me
Before during and after
Make me laugh
Even when the bills arrive
Tell me everything's gonna be alright
Even if you don't know how
Tell me how lucky you are to have me
And I will do the same
Romeo! Romeo!
Get a bloody move on . . .

M Deuchars

ENGAGING THOUGHTS
(Dedicated to Carl)

The day you came into my world you made my life complete,
no other day of happiness ever could compete.
You've brought a light to my soul that glows on every day,
the flame just keeps on flickering and brings a warmth my way.

You will never understand the love I hold in my heart for you,
you think you know how much I care but you haven't got a clue.
You can never know the way I feel, three words will never explain,
'I love you' is so easy to say and I can say it again and again.

But the feelings that I have for you grow stronger every day
and just to know you're near me simply takes my breath away.
To feel your lips upon me when our bodies are entwined,
to feel your touch upon my skin sends a shiver down my spine.

To hear your voice on the telephone when our work insists we part,
brings a smile upon my solemn face and soothes my aching heart.
So when the day comes to wear that ring I'll want to shout out loud,
that I'm engaged to the man I love and I've never been as proud.

Alison Jane Lewcock

THE BYSTANDER

Nowhere to run, nowhere to hide
Filled with contempt and arrogant pride
Locked in confusion wanting to yell
No good crying innocent - I'm guilty as hell!
I stood there and watched, with excitement I cheered
Not knowing why it was him that they feared.
My hands start to shake, the tears start to flow
Something was wrong, but what - I don't know!
A man had just died and darkness closed in
My heart madly thumping, so frightened within
I stood from afar my head bowed in shame
I'd witnessed a killing, so many to blame.
I ran from the crowd, their noise pierced my ears
The courage I had, gave way to my fears.
What can I do? Where can I go?
But to hope for forgiveness for - I didn't know!

Rita Smith

EVERY POEM

Every poem has a reason because it's written from the heart.
It brings someone together, or helps when they are apart.
Sometimes it cheers a sadness, or cheers somebody too,
It can even bring some laughter, if only to a few.
Poems need a lot of thinking, and sometimes does take time,
To try and find the right word, and also make it rhyme.
You share your dreams and imaginations on many many things,
And hope when someone reads it, they too will find a memory to cling.
Every poem has a character of its very own.
Yet when it's read by others, it makes you feel well known.
Just take a pen to paper, choose something from real life,
For every poem written, releases a kind of strife.
Anyone can do it, if only they would try.
Gives vent to lots of feeling, can sometimes make you cry
Every poem that you write, also gives you joy
Also lots of pleasure which no poem can destroy.
It doesn't cost any money to form a little verse
For every little poem gets better , never worse
And when your getting older and your brains are not quite so fast,
Every little poem - reminds you of the past!

Peggy Dugdale

THROUGH THE MISTS OF TIME

A Cornish day, a Cornish sky and Cornish rain in the air,
The children were waiting, their banners inflating - were you there?
Were you there to see St Rumon arrive in a Cornish cove
As he had done in the mists of time, his hands upraised in love?

Then, for a magic moment, was it real or were we dreaming?
Could we hear the ancient music? See the children, banners streaming?
Were we there in Celtic dreamland - was it me and was it you
Swept back through the swirl of years to this land when nearly new?

And did you feel a presence in Churches and Chapel that day?
Did the blessings of Rumon go with us on our wet and muddy way?
For some there were among us rooted deep in the Cornish earth,
But all could sense their history who British are by birth.

It was our day - St Rumon's Day - for Cornish new and old,
Perhaps in another thousand years our story will be told.
For a race of beautiful people in a world we shall never see,
May, like us, for a mystical moment, link their souls with their ancestry.

Anne James

ASHTRAY

He put down the ashtray,
never smoked but nearly choked
that was yesterday;
Someone walked in and found
the scene that he had left,
the ashtray on the ground
sorry no more bets.
Pieces of china were broke
with pills to ease the pain,
this isn't the man that I know
outside it started to rain,
soaked head to foot by their tears,
sorry for lack of goodbyes
with care you'll go on for years
the emptiness made the room cry.
Buried at sea by his past
the cigarette stain like a wound,
an ashtray that he'd built to last
outlived by smoke in the room.

Lefort

THE THAMES TRAMP

Why do you pass me as you walk by the Thames,
with barely a glance my way?
Is it because I'm unwashed and gross in my build,
and you're worried about what I might say?
Is it because I've a hole in my trousers,
and you're frightened at what might peep through?
There's a rip in my jersey, I don't have a coat,
and the sole flaps loose from my shoe.
I sit by the Boathouse in rain and in sun
whilst races are held at great pace,
But the crew never seem to notice me there -
if just one had a smile on his face,
Or tipped me a wink, or said that I stink,
I'd at least have a friend in the place.

The mums and the dads all rush quickly past,
they're worried I'll call out, or touch,
I wouldn't, you know, but the time drags so slow,
and I long for a kind word so much.
I know I'm a sight and must give them a fright,
but there's no other way it can be,
For my home is a den of papers and wood, by the Thames,
with the rats running free.
The howls from the wind entertain me at night,
so what need have I for TV,
But a smile or a nod, or a wave of the hand,
would be enough to satisfy me.

So next time you take your dog for a walk
and see me hunched by that table,
Don't bother to stop - couldn't take up your time -
but notice me, if you are able.

Then for the rest of the day as my cold feet I stamp,
a warm glow will start to spread,
I've been noticed at last,
I'm not really a tramp,
And forget that paper's my bed.

Carole Murphy

MY PERFECT DAY

A beautiful day with a bright blue sky,
Small fluffy clouds pass slowly by,
Down to the beach with its clean golden sand,
My beachmat and towel clutched in my hand,
I swim in the water so cool and clear,
While small shoals of fish come quite near,
As I swim towards them suddenly go,
Quickly darting to and fro,
A yacht sails by so majestic it seems,
As its chrome in the sun shimmers and gleams,
Its sails fully blown like a huge ball gown,
Till suddenly they sag as the wind dies down,
I float on my back in the sun kissed sea,
And let the waves wash over me,
The gulls overhead they screech and scream,
Awaking me from my floating dream,
Refreshed by my swim I head back to shore,
And feel the sand under my feet once more,
The sky suddenly turns to an ominous grey,
An abrupt end to a perfect day,
The wind starts to blow and whips up the sea,
I pick up my things and head home for tea.

Joan Mayer

RECEPTIONISTS IN WAITING ROOMS

Shattered prisms
Make battered prisons
In the tattered waiting room.
And in the gloomy shaded light
Though some don't care how they fare,
I nervously inhale my pipe,
And expel it into the gloom.
Some prisms reflect their awful plight.

And secretary birds,
With see-through smile,
Flash silently past on tinctured tile.
She's glimpsed the secret on the file,
That tells her two and two make three,
And the chars and teasmades all agree.

And as her boots slide over the floor,
Past waiting room to sacred door,
Sometimes she'll get a glimpse through gap,
That tells her this and tells her that.

Like cleaning ladies, security man,
She'll get some sketch of the boss's plan.
But the waiting room people she will fob off,
She wants to keep her job.

Some day your turn will come to wait,
That's when you'll know how we all feel,
That's when your fancy clothes won't rate,
That's when your boot will come to heel!

John Jeffrey Howie

THE DIAMOND JUBILEE

On the 26th of June
It was the Queen we went to see,
When the WRVS celebrated
Their Diamond Jubilee!

We all went to the Milton House
This took us all, much time,
We all dressed, in our Sunday best
Hoped the weather would be fine.

It rained whilst we were travelling
Frequently when there,
The three thousand that attended
Thought this wasn't really fair.

Later in the afternoon
We all crowded round to see,
The cutting of the cake because
The Queen was cutting it, you see.

The crowd it was so dense though
I could not see the cake,
It's been cut and handed out I thought
Again I am too late.
I've missed out having a slice myself
There's been a great mistake!

But I saw the cake cut by the Queen
I was in plenty of time.
I went on to buy a diary
For next year - ninety-nine!
Just hoping I shall still be here
To use it - when it's time!

Ann Saxty

ALONE

It started one February,
when the flowers and hearts were full,
and angels of white were leaving,
inducing streaks of warm-felt sun.
The daylight streamed on through the curtains
and with it brought my usual smile,
but as I reached over to say good morning,
he wasn't there by my side.
I sat up alone and called his name,
the name I'd loved so dearly,
and he was sitting alone downstairs,
looking like he was dreaming.
I pulled the warm gown round my shoulders
and tied it very tightly,
as if longing for some support
as my heart sank with thoughts impending.
'What's the matter?' I simply urged,
with gasps of utmost wonder,
something deeply was on his mind,
he looked at me with eyes of thunder.
'I don't know how to say this,'
his eyes were ringing with flames,
'I can't be with you any longer,
I'm so sorry for the pain.'
My life just flashed before my eyes
and panic took hold of every sense,
I slumped upon the carpet floor,
and asked why with a thousand strengths.
No matter what the man did say -
I heard no real retorts,
explanations are never enough
when your heart is ripped by thoughts.

He left that day, head bowed down low,
a few bags with our things inside,
and never had I been so alone,
truly rejected with banished pride.
I dropped my head and failed to rise,
until strength from somewhere did shake,
the last moment I remember before my wake
was a vision of him and her, not me.
A moment I remember once long ago,
one fresh Valentine's morn,
the sun was streaking through the curtains
and me, in bed, alone.

Cath Spooner

BROKEN SPIRIT

Don't let those fearful eyes, freeze and torture endlessly
So dark lifeless full of pain
Keeping hidden out of shame
Sneaking through the darkened night
Lonely, desperate, without fight.
Memories crowding your whirling head,
Trying to remember what was said.
Holding together shredded clothes
Bloodstained hands and broken nose.
Legs wobbling from the strain
Thunder clatters and lightning flashes
Bringing in the stormy rain
Unbelievable it may be but please come and confide in me.
Don't let those fearful eyes, freeze and torture endlessly.

Pamela Buxton

A Lover's Lament

For one, brief moment, Paradise was ours to hold.
I vowed that you and I would love for evermore,
Oh love! My love, the truth, we know it must be told,
And on that Paradise we must forever close the door.

The sky is darker now my Dearest Heart.
The low-slung clouds portray the depths of my despair.
To know, too soon, so soon we were to part,
When I had come to love you and to really care.

No more to see the sweetness of your smile.
No more to feel the arms
That held me in a warm embrace.
No more to sit and muse with you awhile.
No more my nights enlightened by
The presence of your grace.

Farewell then, Dearest One, I love you still.
The interlude is over now,
No bitterness I feel although we part.
I've treasured moments that I've shared
With you and always will.
Search on for happiness and
Do not heed my broken heart.

V R Broster

7, All Saints' Passage, Cambridge

A publisher's office is geared to enhance
both learning and profits, a civilised stand.

And the goal of the efforts of this versatile team
is a meaningful relation of man and machine.

An author seeks fan mail, then rejoicing departs,
to cruise downtown bookshops, or take lunch at the Arts.

While the Managing Director plays musical chairs:
each day a new desk, or he's wandered upstairs.

In view of the neighbouring School of Divinity,
and chocolates deluxe found in easy proximity.

With these earthly delights and a foretaste of heaven,
what right-minded person could forget number seven?

Elizabeth Moberly

THE WEDDING

The day of the wedding is here
Of son and wife to be
Months of preparations it seems
Has flown so rapidly

'It's raining cats and dogs outside'
Said son 'We'll all get wet!'
'It may stop soon,' I say to him
'The sun will shine I bet.'

We rush to get into the car
It's like Niagara Falls
'Oh no, Dad, turn back quick please do
I've left the rings indoors!'

We're on our way and going fine
Oh crumbs a road block now
'We will be late,' son cries to Dad
'Please get us there somehow.'

At last we're there and see the bride
As lovely as can be
They take their vows the sun comes out
Now proud parents, are we.

Norma Thorpe

SALAD DAYS

Allotments are delightful, enjoyed by us long ago
Working hard to grow some food
With fork, spade and hoe.
Runner beans, scarlet against the fence,
Rows of carrots and beet.
Gooseberries, rhubarb, old wooden bench
Where all the children would meet.
Rose covered shed, rough, made of planks
Where Father would store all his tools.
Where the men would gather when rain came down,
Sitting on wooden stools.
Marigold, pansy, wallflowers too,
Were mixed in with the veg,
The men called to each other across the plots
A good row of peas there 'our Reg'
Cutting a cabbage, flowers for Mum,
The men would go for a drink,
Children would dawdle homewards
Our 'salad days' gone in a wink.

P Knowles

FAMINE

Never has a scene
Left me so depressed,
As to watch a baby suckling
A mother's empty breast.

The place Sudan, the time right now
No food or water there,
Everyone is suffering
A country of despair.

These people need more help
Than mere mortals can provide,
They need a stronger power
Acting on their side.

Lord please help these people
Give them a helping hand,
Let them know that one day
They will walk your promised land.

F England

BURNING BUSH SYMPHONY

The highest fragile violin notes announce a newer dawn
than was before, for this is sacred, holy ground.
And as I close my eyes, I see the faintest glimmer of a newer sun
at a horizon caressing meadows, hilltops, mounds
and valleys with a velvet, gentle gesture of a hand.
The fire in the fingers, held in reserve, the tension latent . . .

And higher rises now the sun and flutes now join
with violins the sounds of early singing birds.
A tremor rises in my soul, rebuilding Healer of the ruins,
left after that violent devastation. You stir
the healing leaves of life upon this deeply rooted tree.
Such defiant physis against discordant unreality.

Oboes and cellos enter in, the warmth of brass upon my skin
which reaches down and penetrates my marrow.
And slowly as it peels away each layer from within,
I stand exposed and naked; but in my open hands, my sorrow.
The drummer's rhythm thunders on, the heat is rising higher,
Your powerful fingers touch my naked I, my God,
                              I am . . . on fire!

Olga Allen

My Life

You gave me life
You also gave me strife
With smacks and slaps
You always used the straps
Abuse and put downs were all I got
Did I deserve them? I did not
My bones were broken
Of the abuse I was not outspoken
Even your brothers got in on the act
You could not deny the fact
As you were sometimes there
Of my feelings you didn't care
You encouraged me to go to his arms
I even fell for his charms
As you both told me this was love
I believed that it was love
Now I know that it was lust
And for you it was a must
Love is an emotion
Not just nocturnal motion
I'm married now to a man you see
Who taught me what love can be
And now it is not fair
To trouble the man for whom I care

Paul Chapman

LAYMAN'S OPINION

Tessa the suppressor
was a fast undresser,
she made the guys pant and pounce,
but little did they know
that many years ago
she filed her love to accounts.

Tessa the suppressor
of sexual fame
didn't let the boys know her runs,
they didn't know from where she came
or whether she still comes.

Tessa the suppressor
hides her heart
whilst hitching up her skirt,
. . . but with frills laid bare
of thrills take care,
for Tessa's just a tart!

. . . but Tessa the suppressor
has much love to give
which she knows just can't return . . .
that's why she plays the field
of highest yield
with boys of no concern . . .

Tricia Nolan

THIS IS OUR TIME

Never stop to contemplate
yesterday's sweet sorrow.
Dare not to procrastinate
living for tomorrow.

It's wrong to dwell, as time will tell,
on mistakes one made in youth.
Let the future serve you well,
seek instead love's truth.

Dreams are often broken, torn;
never have a care.
One day you'll be certain, sure;
permanence to share.

Heartbreak's only lessons learned,
though disappointments shatter,
Use them wisely, standing firm,
then they needn't matter.

Of course, the sands of time still flow,
as they always will:
For it isn't time that's moving fast,
it's us that's standing still.

Trevor F Woollacott

Autumn

As we approach the end of the year
Autumn is here with its abundance of cheer
The trees are clothed with a red, golden glow
Giving a glimpse of heaven's glory below.

The bulbs are all planted in their dark earthen bed
With God's promise of beauty in the days ahead.
Conkers and chestnuts are excitedly found
As small boys and girls scramble around on the ground.

The squirrels collect food in the woodland and park.
Maybe they've heard of Noah's ark.
The gardener tidies the herbaceous border
Leaving the garden tidy and in order.

The debris rots down in the compost bin
For to waste it would be a sin.
Glistening cobwebs on the lawn and the shrub
Transforming with beauty the old flower tub.

Muffins and crumpets for tea by the fire
What comfort and bliss could one more desire.
Birds migrate to lands far away
Others fly in for their winter stay.

Carnival time is here again
Thousands brave the fog and the rain
Tableaus are decked in all their glory
Portraying with splendour their fable or story.

As our life comes to its autumn days
We look back with gratitude and praise
At the way our Lord has led us through
To unknown paths and pastures new.
Secure in the knowledge that he will stay
And guide us safely the rest of the way.

Phyllis Gage

Abandoned

With a look of sympathy and a tender touch,
I softly step forward and reach to pick up,
The shattered pieces of a fragile heart,
Strewn through space and time, ripped apart.

I kneel down willingly, attempting to restore,
The fragmented remains, into a picture of hope,
But pieces lie hidden, lost, unrecoverable,
And I gaze at you through an invisible wall.

As I wait in the shadows, hoping soon they will fade,
I'm perturbed by a figure, emerging from the light of day,
She takes your hand lovingly, and leads you out,
From the darkness which you once felt surround.

Now I am left in your lonely cavern of loss,
The light grows dim, to my cries you give no response,
Haunted by your ghosts, they slowly reach in,
With cold, grey hands, to my heart deep within.

I started out, with love to gain,
To heal and comfort, to end your pain,
But the tables turned and now I'm left stranded,
Feeling your loss, alone and abandoned.

Andrea Smith

NATIONAL LOTTERY

Birthdays of daughters,
Birthdays of sons,
Birthdays of fathers,
Birthdays of mums.

Numbers on houses,
Where they lived once before,
Made out of plastic,
Screwed to the door.
Where they were born,
Or maybe conceived.
These numbers are lucky?
Or so they believe.

Some try the numbers
Picked out of a hat.
And it only takes six to win
The big prize; the millions,
That paper so crisp.
But you might as well chase
The Will o' the Wisp.

Just sit back and listen,
To a miser like me.
Place your pound on number one,
And when the others have nothin',
You'll be the one that's won.

For life is a lottery, and you are the stake,
And it's not what you win,
But what you take.

Bill Bright

UNTITLED

When a (so-called) friend
Broke a leg
My offer of help
Was swiftly sent.
Now! Pushing a wheelchair
Is not all it seems,
The one who sits
Feels quite serene,
The 'learner' who pushes
Has a lot on her mind,
Oh! Why did I offer?
(My reasons were kind).
There's so much advice
to the poor soul who 'drives' -
'That's not the way!
There's no ramp here!
No *stop!*
We must wait till the
road is clear.'
I was a foolish woman -
Willing, but dense,
At *my* age I should have
More common-sense!

Joyce Humphrey

ROBBING THE KESTREL'S NEST

I did not intend them to die
Or even want to see them fly.
Only one egg, t'would not be missed
Think of a cuckoo's rampaging list.

So as the smallest of the gang
Over the rocky ledge did hang
Securing lengths of hangman's rope
Allowing bigger bullyboys more scope.

No coloured smooth eggs nestled there
But savage chicks grotesque and bare,
Devouring dispassionately, mid ravenous shrieks;
Goiterous glistening eyes, cavernous beaks.

'Runts; told us wrong, the twisting cheat.'
Poor unformed wings tried hard to beat.
Cries of desperate protest went unheard
Alas, I could not save that ugly bird.

Reaching, stretching too far I fell
Down, down, down to the gates of hell.
Joining mutilated fledgling remains
I cried not for my aches and pains.

'You're a silly fool,' the leader said,
'For leaving your tea of jam and bread.'
Painfully following that homeward track
Too scared to run, or yet look back.

Thunder claps: disturbed darkest night,
Rhythmic beatings: wings of fervid flight.
Clammy grips: nightmare's fearsome shock,
Awesome awaiting: Judgement: avenging Roc.

H D Hensman

LIFE'S DESTINY

For all the learned prose
and intellect expressed.
In printed page there shows
the lack that it suggests.

It is not just the written word
but lurking in the midst.
A phantom, unseen, unheard,
the importance that is missed.

For all is but in vain
of pride and learnedness
that mortals ever gain,
should they in truth not rest.

The flesh appears so weak
for all the world to see.
Its passing short and fleet
without immortality.

Should humans grasp and hold
their future destiny with
knowledge sure and bold
of life's infinity.

Not just decay and dust remain
but hovering like a dove,
from ashes left behind
the everlasting love.

Whatever has been sown
the fruits to surely reap.
Fulfilment Christ has shown
is in God's hand to keep.

Phoebe J Laing

How Do I Answer?

How do I answer when you ask me
What is the world coming to?
I know in some ways it's better
But there are many rights overdue,
Oh yes, there have been many advances
In medicine, travel and air space,
And the masses are now educated
But the world is not a better place,
There is cruelty still with animals
Vivisection and the factory farm,
Still muggings and fears for old folk
And oft-times babies meet with harm,
Violence on the increase, wars never cease
All walks in life believe in greed,
And the people cry out for peace
Seems there is little faith or creed,
And with technology can be error
Such marvels the world has never seen,
But what of unhappiness and terror
They say, well that has always been,
And there are those who meet and call
For a free and moralistic world,
They say, that goodwill can conquer all
As yet, that banner remains still unfurled.

Jo Rosson Gaskin

DRACULA'S BRIDE

She walks silent in an overgrown park,
Walking to be with her lord of the dark.
The graves peep over the long grass,
In this dead ground, darkness is vast.
She walks in black, one with the night,
Yet in her eyes sparkles of light.
The sparkle of evil that lights her soul,
As she walks among the dead to her goal.

He stands by his tomb, arms held wide
From his lady he will not hide.
His cloak flutters but the night is still,
His white teeth glisten, ready to kill.
For this night he will meet his bride,
And together in darkness they will hide.
Long he has waited for this to come,
Transfixed in him she cannot run.

So in a place of death, lovers meet
And into his arms, lovers greet.
His teeth sink beneath her skin
For now the virgin is ready for sin.
The blood runs down in two streams
And here begins eternal dreams.
Eternal darkness from light to hide
For now Dracula has his bride.

Kirstie Clark

DEATH OF AN ORANGE-PICKER

Stetson on head,
Pulled low over eyes
And two blue steel Navy colts,
Tied to each thigh.
Poncho flicked over shoulder,
To free both his arms,
Elbows turned inwards,
So pistols meet palms.

The doors swing behind him,
The saloon becomes still.
Fears frozen on faces,
Who will he kill?
A flash of gunfire.
A bullet drilled between teeth
One minute an outlaw,
Now a corpse at his feet.

Mr Sudden Death spits,
He looks like he's bored,
He heads for the jailhouse,
To collect his reward.
He nods at the lawman,
'This is Emilio Del Sonte.'
'Nope,' said the sheriff,
'That's The Man from Del Monte.'

Martin Clarke

WHY IS IT?

Why is it, when we go out without a mac, it pours with rain?
Why is it, when we don't take our pain-killers, we are in pain?
Why is it, when we go shopping we forget the number of the bus?
We try to shrug it off without a lot of fuss.
Why is it we are sometimes deaf, we only hear what we want to hear?
Why is it sometimes we don't want to be heard
Then we sneeze or cough?
Why is it when we call the dog to heel, it's off like a shot?
Why is when we've tidied up, the next day it's gone to pot?
Why is it when you bake a cake, it sinks in the middle?
Why is it when you try to pull off a deal
People think you are on the fiddle?
Why is it when the washing's in the machine, off goes the power?
Why is it when the washing's on the line, down comes a shower?
Why is it when you want a bath, there's no hot water?
Why is it when you're old, people think you have plenty of money?
Being old is not sweet as honey or very funny.
Why is it when we are in a hurry, there is always a queue?
Oh dear, why is it in all my eighty years
There is still that question 'Why is it . . .'

Olive Wright

STANDING IN THE NEED OF PRAYER

Large eyes, arrested by their gaze
In apathy, you raise them where you lie
Another face in the parade before me
That daily circles, endless, its way by.

Rustling, movement in the doorway
A hand reaches from your world to mine
Far too polite to frown at the intrusion
I'm free with money, but stringent with my time

Alone you sit, unknown amongst the nameless
I avert my gaze, another love has died
Thinking of you, resonant in your loneliness
I was almost, almost moved to cry.

Deborah Davis

BILLY MOORE

Our unit advanced with crashing sound,
Shells exploding all around.
In my ears I heard someone say,
'It's heavier here than yesterday.'

Guns explode I smell the smoke,
I can't get out I'm beginning to choke.
I see flames and hear another bang,
Then I see an outstretched hand.

I clamber out my tank of death,
And wait for others with bated breath.
Small explosions I hear inside,
No one else came out alive.

We sat and drank a cup of tea,
Me thanking him, he smiling at me.
His name was Billy from a town down south,
He had big blue eyes and a smiling mouth.

I hear firing start up around the bend,
In the confusion I lose my friend.
I shout my sergeant 'Have you seen Billy Moore?'
He said he had been killed the day before.

John Hewins

The Granite Mariner

I walked along the shore one night
With no mortal soul in sight.
There a granite mariner stands
Staring out across the sands.
He and I we stood alone
And I spoke with that man of stone.

Of daring rescues he did tell
By fisher-folk that here did dwell.
Of gale-lashed launchings in the night
And safe return by morning light.
Elated they returned to shore
With ship-wreaked seamen safe once more.

The call to duty came once more,
Menfolk hurried towards the shore
No thought of nation, colour, creed,
Just of sailors in urgent need.
In their hearts no selfish thoughts repose
As they prepared to meet the foe.

The cox'n, Johnson was his name,
Sailed into that foaming main.
The sea with murderous fury rose
As into Eternity they rowed.
Women and children wait in vain,
Widows and orphans they became.

O God, why should those men so brave
End their days in a watery grave?
While experts solemnly proclaim
Safe boats to be their future aim.
And from the deep their souls in anguish cry
Why should the price of progress be so high?

Frank Schofield

NIGHTMARE

Spotlighted in the chair arraigned to face an inquisition,
such meagre knowledge I have gained for public exhibition,
I sit within a cone of light confronting my tormentor
too late reflecting on my haste a knowledge test to enter.
'Your name and occupation, please' - I mop the fevered brow,
'Your general knowledge questions for two minutes, starting now.
Which books are known as the Pentateuch?'
    - my hands are gripping the seat.
'Who was it they called the Iron Duke?'
    - O, one at a time, I entreat.
'Where might you see a meniscus?
What is known as the Heaviside Layer?
What's the meaning of nulli secundus?
Name the author of Vanity Fair.'
    - O vanity, the insanity that brought me to this chair.
'What sort of thing was an arquebus? Who bore old Isaac twins?
What caused the fall of Icarus? Name three of the deadly sins.'
    - O Lord, would thou this penance end henceforth I will my ways amend.
'Who said, *To thine own self be true*? Who led the plot against Caesar?
How much is a sou? Who invented the screw?
And where is the Mona Lisa?
In acres how big is a hectare? Of which metals is brass an alloy?
Whose body was dragged by Achilles around the walls of Troy?
In miles per minute give the speed of sound?
Time's up but you may answer.'
My head is shrunk, my mind so blank no answer will recall.
O suffer me to learn my fate and flee this judgement hall.

Wretched and crushed I crave the floor to open and set me free.
Comes the voice once more,
'You made no score. What's the meaning of felo de se?
Of fifty questions you attempted seven and you passed on forty-three.'

Sidney Headley

HEALTH IS WEALTH

I received it in the post last night
From Forward Press, a kind invite
To narrate a story, preferred in rhyme
Three days to catch the post, there's time
I've been working morning, noon and night
But I would find an hour, in verse I'd write.
But the planned jolly tale didn't appear on the page
Instead there were lines of deep-seated rage
So I deleted the lot and started again
The results were the same using paper and pen.
My inner self could now display
Just what it thought of the eleven hour day
On paper it was plain to see
My inner self was very angry.
For the past two years I've kept up this pace
Carefully maintaining the smile on my face.
'Things will ease up' the boss would say
'Can't give you an assistant, but I'll increase your pay.
More staff have arrived in the other sections
But my requests for help were met with rejections.
And I'm weary now of hearing the boss say
'Let Steph solve your problems, she'll save the day.'
then an e-mail arrived from a wise old friend
'Some thoughts on life to you I send
What use can be made of hard-earned wealth
If the wealthy one is without good health'?
Determined to leave work alone for an hour
I immersed myself in healing poetry power
After 60 minutes my verse was no better
So I've just handed in my resignation letter!

Stephanie Bowler

THE ARTIST VERSUS NATURE

The artist and his sable-points unite as one;
there is for them no ghosting counterfeit;
they fuse their wills - strong brief and bold -
till inward sight looks out to hold
a scene unique - with life's evasive Marathon for None.

No summer's indigos shall transgress winners by deceit;
no shadow-handed slight would dare complete - (with cunning
use of thinner's bleach) - a rupture to a canvas that is taut;
nor, with practised excellence, construe a fake
that counts for nil or frigid nought.

The artist may observe a simple flower to paint - a daisy
flaunting dancing grace - to bring new life, without a sigh,
to sketch-page that was blank. He limns a trace with rigger-brush
for floating shade and light, splashing whorls of bright cobalt
to curve an arching sky - then frank the trailing cirrus clouds
with white.

He scythed wide lees with palette-knife to find the meaning
of earth's life. But as he sought to understand his scroll -
(calm-bestowed, unplanned) - nature came and bent his will,
demanding life as toll, or rhythm would be lost. She was mindful
of revenge, and forced his hand to wither summer's warmth - then
seized the stage with winter's biting frost.

She raised an anvil's flattened head - its shadow fell across
the artist's brow - to leave a crest of fear instead.
But a sunlit beam pierced through the storm-tossed clouds -
the artist cast off nature's whispered shrouds, and on the
sketch-pad's vacant page - was burnt the test of nature's rage.

Dorothea Payn Le Sueur

DESPERANDUM - HELP!

Is it that I cannot see it?
Is it that it is not here?
Is it that it's gone forever?
I suspect it is and fear.

I am at a loss, frustrated
Knowing not which way to turn
Is it over? Is it under?
I'm unsure I'll ever learn.

It is hunted with great fervour
In and out and up and down
All I know is all this searching
Is giving me an angry frown.

Three days now I've lispthed my letters
Through the gap that once was filled
With my plate and missing toothlet
(for which the dentist highly billed)

I am now so full of sadness
that I cannot chatter, grin
Without that awful gap appearing
just above my double chin.

I try to smile without exposing
The space where my white tooth should be
And I wonder where I laid it, hid it,
That is one big mystery.

How I long to cry 'Eureka -
I have found my missing plate'
But hopes are fading every minute
and I'm in a right old state.

Joanna Pickett

EMERGENCE

Like an embryo forcing itself from its constraining bubble,
I emerge and find myself standing on a threshold.
What once appeared uniquely the due of others
is summarily too mine to behold.

With stomach a-flutter I revel as the momentous sense of wonder
                                                             envelops me.
It was merely my own private prison in which I languished awhile,
but now I grasp that I am indeed free.

I am dizzy, expectant, light-headed as I step forward into this newly-
                                                            discovered realm.
There are such an endless stream of new horizons awaiting discovery,
with mine own hand at the helm.

Like a tiny new leaf emerging from a branch,
or perhaps a butterfly from its cocoon,
I am seduced by the myriad options which substitute the void.
I accept the sense of rapture at such a diversity of passages with
                                                    which I am so buoyed.

With body all a-tingle, I step forward boldly in time,
knowing all is possible if patience reigns supreme.
Excitedly I venture forth, trust forging a playful smile across my lips,
striding towards my dream.

I jump, I dance, I whirl, I spin, I laugh aloud . . .
I realise I have released myself from the confines of ere.
My joy plain for all to see, I shout out to the world
and loudly announce my accomplishment,
as I have now conquered fear.

Terry Harnwell

GROWING OLD TOGETHER

Through the gathering storm of vagueness
Onward stumble you and I.
I have lost my keys and bus pass,
Hope they'll turn up by and by.

You have just mislaid your cheque book,
So can't pay the butcher's bill -
What is that you say? You've found it
Outside on the window sill?

How the hell would it have got there?
Are we really going mad?
No, we're simply growing older,
Something not entirely bad.

People's names and people's faces
Stubbornly remain apart.
So for fear of looking foolish,
Conversations do not start.

When the day comes when I cannot
Tell you where I parked the car
Then I'll think it's time to pack up
And that things have gone too far.

Nothing matters while I have you,
Pain, nor loss of memory,
Loss of car or loss of money,
While you still remember me.

Roger Plowden

HOLIDAY BLUES

Poppy pussy surveyed the scene,
There was only one thing it could mean.
Bags and cases were everywhere
Holiday time was in the air!

Sister Chloe said not to mind,
The neighbours would be very kind.
But Poppy thought about her tum!
And how she'd really miss her mum.

Tigger said the time would fly
Once the folks had said goodbye.
But Poppy couldn't see just why,
And wandered off, with tearful eye!

But Mum and Dad had done their best,
And neighbours happily did the rest.
Poppy slept and ate just the same,
She even answered to her name!

And sure enough the days slipped by,
With warming sun and clear blue sky.
Until, what joy - Mum's voice is heard
Saying, 'Naughty puss you've killed a bird!'

Poppy stirred - she'd been asleep,
Was it real! Could she bear to peep?
Then Mum was there with a hug and a kiss
The holiday was over - purrfect bliss!

Chris Saunders

I Wish I Could Have Known You

Every picture tells a story but the questions still remain
as I'm looking at your face within this photo frame.
Gathered pieces of a puzzle of the dim and distant past -
dreams that have been broken and a love that didn't last.
A face that holds a smile, I see laughter in your eyes,
but they are shrouded in the sadness of all the tears you've cried.

I know you must have loved him but did he break your heart?
I wonder how you met him, and carried on . . . when your life fell apart.
The pain of a young mother leaving her child behind,
as the cries of her new baby stay forever in her mind.

I don't know your circumstances or why you made that choice -
perhaps my heart can now find peace as you hear my voice.
Your secrets in the darkness hidden deep within your soul,
affect us all, as we each search for part of you to hold.
I wish I could have known you and held you by the hand,
talked in quiet conversations - I would try to understand.
I'm like you, a woman, I sometimes don't know where to turn,
but the choice that took you far away allowed you never to return.

I wish I could have met you, I wonder what we'd say?
I'd tell you that I miss you even more than yesterday.
Questions left unanswered, a story never told,
but as the pieces fit together somehow the truth unfolds.
You're part of who I am today, I'm walking in your shoes,
but if we had the chance to meet what words would I choose?

I'd tell you . . . how your son became a father
with a heart that's pure and true,
How he loves the girl he married, how he looks so much like you.
How he's sacrificed for many years, so I might understand
what it is to know a father's love - a gentle, guiding hand.

I know you would be proud of him if you saw him today,
but if we had the chance to meet I wonder what we'd say?
I wouldn't chastise you or say your choice was wrong,
although your pain has bound our hearts in chains for far too long.
I've worn this hurt around my heart, I've held on to my pain,
but there would be no anger - no more need to caution blame.

I wish I could have known you, even now I miss you still -
I'd tell you that I love you . . . and that I always will
You're a treasure that I'll hold forever in my heart
and even though we never met, we'll never be apart
But most of all I'd want to say that after all these years,
forgiveness is my gift to you . . . it's written in these tears . . .

Keren Newth

I'M GLAD WE MET

When we first met it was really strange
me recovering from an operation
our partners were colleagues from work
we seemed to hit it off straight away
little did we know that circumstances
would throw us together so fast
we lived a lifetime's emotions in a few years
I don't think we missed one emotion
but all it did was make us closer
'your daughter's birth'
was one of the happiest
life defiantly tried us
but we are always there for each other
you became more than a friend
you became part of my family

Paula E Jones

Untitled

She was a girl whose mind was fed by books and by computers
Honed to perfection by the skills of academia's tutors.
With heavy backpack, carefully planned, she meant to travel far,
For she would seek her place of dreams, the land of Shangri-La.

She hitched and trudged through foreign lands with aching back
                                                and feet,
Enduring the experience of sand, and flies, and heat.
In each new place she quickly learned one cannot judge by looks,
She waited tables, cleaned out rooms and helped abusive cooks.

But on she went believing that her karma lay afar
Where peace and happiness abound, the land of Shangri-La.
For three long years she journeyed on (what stories she could tell)
Through India and Africa, America as well.

A woman now and worldly-wise, she thought she'd visit home,
To see the land she'd left behind when starting out to roam.
Her dad was at the airport, his prodigal he'd found,
She saw the fields and village, amazed, she gazed around.

Familiar sights and sounds awoke her memories of yore,
She had returned. This was her home. She knew she'd roam no more.
For home is where the heart is, so if that is where you are,
There is no need to try to find the land of Shangri-La.

E Hollihead

Payback Story

A weekend of fun and glory
Starts the payback story
Stay in surroundings new
With music, drink and friends too
Do some things too crazy to mention
Lucky not to be held in detention.

Home again the world to face
Is bad enough but to race
To a stop and fall ill
Time to take another pill
Lying on the couch so hot
Feeling like my brain's ready to rot.

Getting better, reality to deal with now
It's been too long, I don't know how.

Thomas P Brown

NIGHTMARE

She rises from my dream
Enveloped in light
A kiss so warm, so sweet
In the coldness of the night
A bitter taste of loneliness
The nightmare starts again
As I fight to find the reason
Which is causing so much pain.

Now as she glides towards me
Setting fire to my soul
From my memory, grows a meaning
Searching blind into the cold
My life's the empty darkness
And the lady not a ghost
But the one who was my everything
The one that I loved most.

Oh how I wish, it could be her
And not the light of day
That wakes me from my vision
As the nightmare fades away.

Barnaby Newman

Don't Look At My Clothes, Look At Me

I beg of you, please help me
Share with me, a penny or two
I'm homeless and I am so cold
Even a hot drink would do

I am capable of work and trust
But they just do not want to know
To prove myself, I beg, you must
Give me the chance and I will show

I got no love from Mum and Dad
They abused me then threw me out
I need your help I am so cold and sad
I'm tired and so down-and-out

I feel so rejected and it's just not right
Please anyone out there what can I do?
I want a warm bed to sleep in at night
I want to be loved just like you

The next time you see me
With head hung in shame
Remember we are all God's children
And that I am not all to blame.

Katina Hilliard Sharpe

DEATH

The breath of life,
No longer there,
No more that earthly smile,
Instead a calm tranquillity,
That makes it all worthwhile.

Life does not end,
With our last breath,
It simply moves along,
To something warm and wonderful,
Like angels singing songs.

Before we're born,
There is no life,
Until that angel's kiss,
That stirs our heart,
And fills our lungs,
We can't remember this.

Why be afraid,
We cannot know,
If death has any sting,
Or if we simply float away,
Upon an angel's wing.

Lez Walsworth

ROAD TO RECOVERY

The man who cries himself to sleep,
Is the child, who long ago,
Held back his tears, refused to weep
And never told a soul.

The man who tears himself apart,
Is the child who could not tell,
He kept it secret from the start,
Was told he'd burn in hell.

The man who cannot face his friends,
Is the child who played alone,
Wishing that his world would mend
And he was safe, at home.

The man who's had enough of lies,
Is the child who wants what's right.
He needs to shout those silent cries,
He made alone at night.

The man who's fighting for his mind,
Is the child who was confused,
Were all his family really blind,
To the fact he was abused?

The man who's going to win this fight,
Is the child whose strength ensured,
That he could love with all his might,
Despite what he'd endured.

The man who smiles and grasps my hand,
Is the child who's found the key.
He's come to know, to understand,
What childhood should have been.

J L M

WE ALL FELL DOWN THE STAIRS

The bruises fade
Still the pain never goes away
'You need some discipline'
That's what my father used to say.

He needed some space
I got under his feet
With so many children crying at night
It's hard to be heard on this street.

It's got nothing to do with anyone else
He'll raise his kids
The way he sees fit
It's to make the child stronger
'It's for your own good
So don't you forget it.'

Mum says 'Not now Dear,
You know how upset your father becomes
When you moan.'
Stand back and do nothing
Has become the motto in this home.

I can hear the shouting in the next room
The caring neighbours can hear it as well
Those curtains twitch then suddenly close
Nobody wants to get involved in this domestic hell.

It happens every day all over the world
I pray to God that someone cares
Don't let it be a part of everyday life
We're the children who fell down the stairs.

Sean Brown

THE REMAINS OF EACH DAY

A fly takes a little bite
        which is followed by another
the flies seem rampant
        each has a little brother

Little weakened cherubs
        victims with ebony skin
every day is a struggle
        not much flesh beneath the skin

The land is harsh and dry
        the soil is but a sea of dust
fresh mounds are made each day
        to avoid disease they must

Few tears are ever shed
        upon the money that will die
it would be a waste of energy
        most are too weak to cry

A vulture swoops overhead
        eating morsels by the hour
other scavengers move in
        with beaks of awesome power

Who are the likes of us
        to be unhappy with our lot
theirs is a death sentence
        how much time have we got?

Trevor Vincent

TO ALL THE ANNA KARENIAS OF THE WORLD

Who had bitter affairs
Betraying their husbands
Feeling guilt and remorse only, after

Their husbands
Utterly shattered and dismayed
At such concealed deception
Are torn between reason and passion
Seeing a child is involved
Whose interest
Are they more concerned about

The love triangle
Has become dual broken hearts
Her bit of fun
Has disappeared
Leaving her empty and dejected

While her husband
Doesn't want to know
Taking the fools' way
She contemplates suicide
While the husband's name
Is in shame and tatters

Realising she's done the worst
Seeing it's for the best
She runs
And leaves.

Tahira

Never Too Late

They keep telling me I'm much too old,
And I know my hair is no longer gold,
I should remember that I am now sixty
Refrain very definitely from doing things risky.
I started to think time was not on my side
So decided to take a promised balloon ride,
No sooner said, but there and then booked
Although seven in the morning still I was hooked.
Gliding and drifting way up in the sky
Watching the Suffolk countryside float by
Dry champagne at nine couldn't lift spirits higher
So what if I'm playing with that old hell fire.

My ambition list is getting slowly crossed through
I've done tea at the Ritz, ten-pin bowling too,
Visited China to see the Great Wall's might
Been on safari, taken a microlight flight.
Last year I made a tandem parachute jump,
The free fall bit did make the heart thump,
But I loved every single blissful second
And what if the Grim Reaper had beckoned,
I'd have said with a wry smile
At least I shall go out in style -
But would you mind waiting just as little bit longer
Cos my desire for an airship flight gets ever stronger.

I feel more alive now then when I was twenty,
There's things to do and places to visit aplenty.
I may be a 'mouldy' and well past my prime
But I'm still making the very most of my time.
So look out world I've not done with you yet
There's life in the old dog still - you bet!

M J Prebble

THE ELOPEMENT OF LADY BETTY CHARTERIS
(An incident related by Captain Gronow in his Reminiscences (1862)

Smitten with the noble lady's charms
The handsome guardsman, proven brave in arms
At Waterloo, and forced by stern Papa
Through lack of funds, to worship from afar,
At London season's end resolved to take
The coach to Scotland, there with haste to make
Attempt to lure his love from family seat.

Disguised in wig and seedy working suit
He reached a nearby village in pursuit
With organ-man and monkey in his train;
Renewing contact with his love again
He urged her to decide elopement day;
For this our dashing hero paved the way
With planned diversion promisingly neat.

While organ-grinder entertained the staff
A chaise and four was hidden by the path;
All prospered till the zealous governess
Beside her lady, cried out in distress
As Andrew sought to pull his love away
And hurry her to where the carriage lay:
'It's now or never, Betty, I entreat!'

Duenna's screams, as clinging to one arm
She strove to save her precious charge from harm,
Alerted staff and father to the foe . . .
Our ardent ensign judged it best to go!
Much mirth was caused in regimental mess,
But Betty's loss did not for long depress:
He'd soon another dulcinea meet!

Dennis Tackley

HOME VILLAGE

The village where I spent my childhood
Is not in existence now
In its place is a green hill covered by trees
The park where we played
A residential garden for three houses
The school still stands
Pupils come from another village
Brought in by bus
To fill the classes we once used
The Co-op and the shop, the two chapels
Demolished, no trace of all the houses
The street lamps where we used to meet
The bus stop where we left the village, no trace
The pit and its iron wheels
The steady drone of coal filled trucks
That filled the village with life
Have been replaced with the quietness and darkness
Of an isolated hamlet
But the people still live on, transplanted into various places
Friendly people with a sense of humour
And a sense of family and community
That the village seems to have had
A population scattered far and wide
Whom when they meet still remember
With fondness where they came from
You can travel far and wide
And yet still meet someone or their cousin
From that small village
And feel happier for that meeting

Joan Smith

ODE TO TEMPING

'Over-worked and under-paid' -
a worker's epitaph!
But no-one seems to spare a thought
for temporary staff -
The ones who don't have pension funds,
whose holidays are few,
Who don't get paid for being sick
like other workers do.
They're sent out on assignments
and required to know the ropes -
All systems must be quickly sussed
or else they're classed as 'dopes'.
A bolder temp will ask for help
but then the air gets tense
And supervisors mutter,
'Oh, good grief! It's common-sense!'
Sometimes, a temp turns up for work
to find the job's no more
The Agency has boobed
so Tempus Fugit's out the door!
That's why *this* temp's snuffed it
and her working days are past
She'll have a great, big headstone that says -
'Permanent, at last!'

Sally Thompson

A Lost Journey

That night to the city of Leeds I went,
To a house on The Avenue, we were sent.
I was so confident that I knew the way,
There was no need, to my Father to pray.
All went well, till we reached the city,
I should have asked, much more the pity.

Soon I was lost, we knew not this place,
Confused and bewildered, so in disgrace.
I asked directions, we searched in vain,
Round and round we went, and back again.
So confused by now, and my time so late,
I rang my son at home, to tell our fate.

I asked him to enquire, the exact place,
If our friend rang, so to ask for grace.
Again we went, to search for the street,
But now it was early, no others to meet.
So it was time, to ring back home again,
I knew that our search, was now in vain.

A telephone I found, down a side street,
So we rang up home, and admitted defeat.
The reply we got, filled me with dismay,
A road off Salisbury Avenue, he did say.
My tears welled up, deep within my eyes,
How could I find it now, my heart cries.

Amid my tears, and a broken heart, I had,
I had failed to ask Jesus, so I was sad.
Then through the windows, I did but see,
The name of this side street, facing me.
Salisbury Avenue, is what my eye espied,
Could this be true, my soul nearly died.

Fred Schofield

UNWELCOME GUEST

We were young, we were broke, and the house was cheap.
Not a mansion of course, just a gloomy old heap.
We painted and patched, hammered nails by the score,
Until all was smart, from the roof to the floor.
Content all our hard work had been for the best,
We snuggled down, safe in our own little nest.

> Then the footsteps began, on the stairs in the night,
> And whispering in corners away from the light.
> A dark filmy shape, by the door in the hall,
> That could be a shadow - or nothing at all.

'We'll ignore it,' we said, 'It will soon go away.'
That was easy to say in the light of the day.
But no comfort when lamps flickered low in each room,
And a grey mist was drifting around in the gloom.
Then came knocking on walls - that's what frightened us most,
We had to admit it, *this house has a ghost.*

> We worked and we saved and our bank balance grew,
> This time we would purchase a house that was *new*.
> No dark creepy corners but airy and light,
> Sun streaming through windows all shiny and bright.

We moved on a spring day, with flowers everywhere,
Our new house was full of the warm scented air.
We sang as we made our home tidy and neat,
Climbed weary to bed when the task was complete,
And sleepily spoke of the peace that would stay
Now our unwelcome guest had been left far away.

> Then we heard it - a soft pit-a-pat on the stair,
> A faint rapid breathing disturbing the air,
> Then a long thankful sigh - of contentment, no less,
> As our ghost settled in at our brand new address.

Audrey Bate

JOEL 2 v 25
SO I WILL RESTORE TO YOU THE YEARS THAT THE SWARMING LOCUST HAS EATEN

No one else could see the wounds
The scars that never healed
Of things that happened years ago
That I can always feel

All those hurts locked up inside
Too painful ever to confide
Loved ones lost, rejection, pain
Would I ever be whole again

People say are you alright
Yes, I say I'm fine
No you're not stop lying
You know inside you're crying

Then Jesus said to me one day
It's time to do some healing
He touched those places exposed and raw
And said those years you lost I will restore

He heals me gently day by day
As we walk hand in hand
It's His love that heals with such precision
He's my Lord my healer and physician.

A Langley

My Garden

As I watch through the window, as the sun goes down,
The heads of the flowers and blooms turn and frown.
The roses bow to the left and the foxgloves to the right,
They chatter to each other all through the night.
A gentle breeze has taken flight, in amongst the trees,
It must be getting stronger, as their branches touch their knees,
The leaves are rustling briskly as three fall to the floor,
Please don't rustle harder, 'cause I don't want anymore.
The grass is looking lush, as the evening dew does fall,
The little plants take shelter as they lean against the wall.
All the tiny plantlets that are planted round the lawn,
Cuddle up together, till the early hours of dawn.
They're looking really tired now, the baskets and the tubs,
But the holly tree looks really well, centred among the shrubs.
And looking at the ivy, I think it's about to die,
Going to Great Ivy Heaven, up there in the sky.
A little lilac sweet-pea is peeping through the privet,
Looking a little closer I can see a white one with it.
There's still a little honeysuckle over by the gate,
I think it must be lonesome as it's blossomed rather late.
There's a bird on our table picking at the bread,
I think that it's a robin, I can see his chest of red.
The bird table stands boldly upright, in amongst the flowers,
I could sit here forever and watch the birds for hours.
The night is drawing in now and the garden is at rest,
I'll look again tomorrow when the blooms are at their best.
The winter's getting closer and the weather it will harden,
Thank you for listening to the story of my little garden.

Margaret Nuttall

AUTUMN

As I sit here lost in the wood,
Lookin' down through the meadow
That once was so good
Broken bare trees that hath leaves do fall
Sat under an oak that once stood so tall
Is a shadow of himself since the
Autumn due call.
But it's nature's due course
The pine tree does fear,
And the almighty force
Whose leaves stood a year,
Clingin' to its life so loyal to its tree
It's now the autumn's knife
Tryin' to cut it free,
But it's only just begun
As I hear the sacred splinter,
Gettin' its work all done
For it's now already winter.

John A McHale

BE LIKE A LION

You thought I was a defect
I know you really did
You never said directly
But in your words it hid

Never believe a label
Attached to anyone
Open your eyes
Use common sense
Don't be like a sheep
Always in a crowd
Bleating, repeating, bleat!

Be like the lion
Who is a king
And therefore uses his own mind
Don't be like the sheep
Who really are quite blind.

Sue Chadwick

THE LETTER ON THE MAT

A letter fell upon the mat from a contact agency
Telling of your search for that person who bore you - Me
I laughed, I danced, I screamed, I cried - at last it was revealed
The dreadful deed so long despised, shame which I've concealed
In parting with my baby boy - so beautiful, innocent and small
A precious gift of life, your soft warmth I still recall
No options left to my lost soul, believing I'd committed sin
From that day I've not been whole, separated wickedly from kin
My son, I gave you to another, at the time I was not able
To be a good and caring mother, pressures forced on me untenable
For thirty years I've lived with regret, each moment filled with pain
Wondering if perhaps you'd seek me out, if I'd see you again
From cruel darkness into light, my destiny uncovered
Doubt, carrying you into sight, my long lost son discovered
Word followed soon, establishing the fact that you were *he*
The wondrous little human being I'd been parted from so cruelly
My soul cannot express the fulfilment on my part
Ending desperation and distress - I'm allowed a brand new start
A longed-for healing meeting - all regretting set aside
The fortuitous and restoring greeting, for which my broken heart
                                                            has paid.

P R McDonald

Boiling Point

simmering below the surface
with subsided rage
boiling point draws nearer
as he slaps her across the face

the temperature is rising
and it's not about to stop
the slap becomes a punch
as he starts to blow his top

boiling point gets nearer
as a man assaults his wife
and in a blaze of desperation
she blindly grabs a knife

boiling point is here
the kettle begins to overflow
she begins to defend herself
matching him blow for blow

two and a half minutes later
with her hands stained with blood
she has reached boiling point
and he never thought she could

Mark Dobbs

THAT SINKING FEELING

A motorway network, with no lorries or cars,
A fantasy space trip, with no Venus or Mars.
To sail for a lifetime, on a sea with no shore,
A life-threatening sickness, with no hope of a cure.

A town with no buildings, just bricks turned to dust,
When you build up a business, and then it 'goes bust'.
A night full of darkness, with no stars and no moon,
An abundance of noise, with no rhythm or tune.

To speed down a hill in a car with no brakes,
No family at Christmas, just a heart full of aches.
To step through a doorway, and find there's no floor,
To be shut in a cell, with no window or door.

Dead silence, no music, in Carnegie Hall,
To wait by the phone, but never a call.
To scorch in the desert, with no trace of shade,
To run out of money, with bills to be paid.

You thought you'd a fortune, when you needed it most,
But your prize-winning coupon got lost in the post.
I knew that feeling, for which no words can be found,
When I found you crying, because I'd let you down.

Ray Baker

The Catch

The woman looked through lashes veiled
Her mechanism never failed
Those powers tested, tried and true
With little help emotions grew

Soft face and form as yet prolong
But gentle mask belies the strong
An armoury no man could find
The weaponry of womankind.

This form perfected on the earth
Will never yet deny her birth
But use those gifts a special way
And once again the man must pay.

With eyes that promise unrevealed
Intentions, gentle flesh to yield
She stands supreme and yet beguiled
This woman flower of nature wild.

The man now drawn magnetically
To take the femininity
His passion soon to take control
And thus she casts his leading role.

Beneath him now she feels his urge
And gently helps new life to surge
Man conquers all with flow and ebb
But it was she who spun the web.

Susan Davis

The Painting

A painting is a pulse of life
Apart from that you live,
The imprint of a person
Who had its scene to give.

A skill, expressed in form
To please another's eye,
The image of a part of time
For you to question why.

A distant brain has guided
The sway of brush, to show,
Line and colour, image
In fascinating glow.

You, posses a part of he
Or she, who lived a spell,
Another life, in vision
With you, or me to dwell.

To inherit, or to buy
Another's part of mind,
And be a little richer
With that, thereon, you find.

If primitive or cultured skill
The seeing is the pleasure.
It's yours to seek the message
Or, scan at varied leisure.

Henry J Green

Exist

Another click of the clock through my mind; how so
To lay, cold, lifeless, no feelings, emotion.
With no life around me, to tell all about me,
The burning, my pain, backwards in motion.
Do I care? No one knows, but I know they're there,
Be it the evil inside, oh, the confusion.
Straight through my skull, into my soul,
Playing the fool to Death's institution.
Whether light or dark, it matters no more,
The blackness, depression, keep perseverance,
Hurry my friend, my enemy haunts me,
The root of bitterness is human existence.
Deeper, further, it is no longer I,
My hands are red, my heart is torn.
Your great mistake, feeding like maggots,
Singing all praises to the unborn.
Sweet tears of anger, malice and hate.
Yet one more path to destruction, and why?
They cling to the inside, no trace on my face,
They sting, they blind my inner eye.
I shout and I scream but the demons just stare.
Where is my guardian angel Endurance?
I haven't been found, a card in a pack,
They like to play dares with my futile occurrence.
The seventh hour, so what does it matter?
I will lay my bones here, waiting to rot.
It's my last hope and it cleaves to my lungs,
This time, once more . . .
Another click of the clock.

Gary Ridley

An Occasional Reminder

A coat as black as night
His body long and lean
Whiskers full of pride
And eyes of emerald green

Impatient cries for love
Once given, turn to glee
And once he's had enough
Impatient to be free

He struts into his kingdom
Open arms he just ignores
His eyes are tired and heavy
He longs to rest his paws

His cushion has been chosen
The new one on the chair
Paws pad and claw the velvet
He's king he doesn't care

He longs to be in slumber
But no, we don't agree
So a playful swipe with claws
Is enough to let him be

A snob you may well call him
Much more than when he came
So an occasional reminder
That *Bumble* is his name.

Debbie Gibson

A Love Unfolds

Two people embrace, a love to unfold,
happiness surrounds them - let's be bold!
Wedded bliss comes round and about,
a new life of sharing a reason to shout.
A home to provide, a living to earn,
togetherness and a family do yearn.

Then suddenly two turns to three,
a new life begins and the couple glee.
Years of pleasure and learning simply soar,
maybe an increase from three to four.
A security surrounds a protective gown,
then the barrier begins to break down.

Out of infancy grows a determined young mind,
those childhood dreams a reality to unwind.
Do you stand by, deter or encourage,
or step aside, let them go, then we need courage!
Part of our lives is drawing away -
a child leaves home, an emptiness comes to stay.

Where stood youth whose clear eyed vision cried,
it's readiness to leave aside.
Life, whose style has love profound,
now stands one eager, in honour, truth justice ground.
A new adventure, a wave to ride,
a way to walk, a dream, a bride?

In each breast, fresh spirits surge,
a tie to cut, new bonds to forge.
A space in which this child may grow,
dreams were made in years now gone.
A search for something to fulfil,
an aching emptiness - is this God's will?

Do we do it now or, wait a while?
Let's rest and see -no -
to wait would just gloom bring,
a live new song our hearts must sing
Fresh summits we will aspire to reach,
new wine to taste, new ways we will teach.

A new beginning is sought a new joy in our hearts,
a joining with God whose love never parts
A time of relaxing in the gift of peace,
a time to share, a time to receive God's love to release.
New sights are focused in a future that's set,
to wipe out our past and allow God to forget.

Two people embrace a love unfolds,
happiness surrounds them as they grow old . . .
Then age grasps an untimely end,
a partner lost an empty aching heart to mend
A time to breathe in all that has lapsed,
caressing the memory of love's eternal cost.

Margaret Webb & Irene Leese

ONE GLASS EYE

I asked him to tell me his story
As I gazed into his eyes,
Knowing his soul would scream the truth
When his lips mouthed painful lies.

'I once was a soldier in foreign lands,
A Captain of courageous men;
I marched them all to the mouth of death
And dragged them back again.

I knew they had full trust in me
And loved me like a god;
They knew I could control their destinies
With a simple nod.

Yet, as a man, I had my faults,
My judgement sometimes failed,
And once I sent my men to die
In a house at the end of a field.

I ordered them to search the place,
Even though I was not sure
If a booby-trap had been set to go off
When they opened the unlocked door.

I saw and heard the bomb explode
As I sat so safe nearby;
One man alone returned alive
With a hole in place of his eye.

It is the man who you see here . . .'
He motioned to his friend.
And as I stared into the eye of glass
I saw where the tale would end.

'I've left the army,' he went on:
'I wasn't fit to lead,
And I feel as if my cares have fled,
Like a prisoner finally freed.'

And this was the lie he uttered
As he struggled to catch his breath;
I could see from the shadow across his brow
That the Captain was close to death:

The life is squeezed from his aching throat
By fingers cold and dry,
For round his neck is the fatal grip
Of a man with one glass eye.

Annie Lovelock

MARCH 13TH

Nobody's going to school today
Now Hamilton's blasted its meaning away.
He took out sixteen with a wave of his gun,
Stole the light from their eyes, bled their smile from the sun.
The town reels, writhing in silent pain,
Nobody thought death would target Dunblane.
Our bodies still function, we breathe as before
But our souls lie bleeding across the gym floor.
Tomorrow hangs heavy with never agains,
With playground kisses and lunchtime amens,
With favourite toys that get in the way,
With birthdays and cuddles and friends round to play.
Still the living go on like mechanical dolls
And learn to survive wearing lives full of holes.

Jill Bramham

Vision

Life's mirror perched upon some wall
will it shatter, will it fall
will it reveal the hidden pain
does it expose the falling rain
that falls in torrents from my eyes
drowning out friendship and flushing out lies.
Will it tell you of all the good
that's gone to waste, if only it could
reflecting on how life ought to be
now you don't want to listen to the likes of me.
So mirror, mirror upon life's wall
take care one day that you don't fall
for your jagged splinters will leave a scar
upon my life and I won't go far
before I'm standing alone in the rain
searching the shadows and calling your name.
And the likes of me is what you had
life's broken mirror, good and bad
tainted friendship held so dear
your voice is loud, but the words aren't clear.

Stephen Keyes

My Baby

Not so long ago you were a baby
Overnight, it seems you're a young lady
You've grown so tall and beautiful
You've started secondary school
Where have all the years gone, I wonder?

You kept me up at night when you were teething
And how sweet you looked as you lay sleeping
I remember your first steps around the furniture
The tears I wiped away when you fell over
Is it all so long ago?

Your first day at school (I was crying)
I missed you from the house there's no denying
You talked non-stop about the teacher
And brought home almost every living creature
It's not so long ago, do you remember?

Now you're twelve years old, quite the young lady
I know you don't think that you're still my baby!
Just remember darling, as you go off to school
I still lay down all the rules
Grown up, not yet, remember there's still a long way to go!

Dorothy Aplin

TEARDROP

A teardrop falls like the first drop of rain,
The skies open up; it is much of the same,
Life and love are behind all the pain,
But still I feel a satisfactory gain.

The shape of the tear is the same as before,
But the reason it's there is for something much more.
My body is unhurt; still my eyes are sore
For it's my emotions that are drained and are kicked to the floor,
You think you're the strongest and are in total control,
But you've no answer and are second to your soul.

A teardrop falls like a crisp flake of snow,
Where it will land nobody knows.
It got lost in the river of hatred and spite.
It tried and tried but was powerless to fight.

Denis Catley

A Synopsis Of The Weather

A synopsis of the weather followed the international news,
a synopsis of the weather wound its mesmerising muse
into an otherwise soundless kitchen;
where breakfast paraphernalia stood, piled neatly,
ready to be put away,
hands that should be transporting them, unmoving lay
solid and cold as the slate grey,
mopped, quarry-tiles that supported them.
Hands, crag'ed as the rugged earth from which the ancient
tiles were hewn,
stilled for an eternity
from the constant motion that had been their normality
since birth unwrapped them from a mother's womb.

A synopsis of the weather found its meditative ruse
fell on frosted eyes, sightless, untwitching,
though the Reyburn, stoked, riddled and filled, glowed beneath
a topped-up copper kettle
of brightly burnished, age-thinned, gleaming metal.
Under a polished fruit-wood settle
hard worm gum boots, carefully placed, waited;
now sated she no longer waited, lone as she in being had done since
companionship passed away,
leaving naught but work's comfort perpetually in motion
t'wards hibernation's rejoining tomb.

A synopsis of the weather followed the international news
into a likewise senseless kitchen . . .

M C Lawrence

DAY AND NIGHT

The tents unzip and out run the four,
they run to the woods to play and explore.
The September sun glistens through the trees
beaming on the small boys' dirty faces and grazed knees.

Jumping, prancing, teasing their friends,
hiding behind trees, in holes and in dens.
Giggles and laughter echo through the wilderness
darkness closes in and light becomes less.

One small boy seems to be left behind,
strange thoughts begin to enter his mind.
Faint sounds rapidly grow louder,
whilst his heartbeat thuds prouder.

Arms around his legs he crouches down,
shaking in the darkness wearing a frown.
The young one stares into the night,
unable to think straight, consumed with fright.

Dried twigs crunch under his tiny feet,
what kind of fate will this boy meet?
Shouts for his friends, then quietly sucks his thumb,
doubtful that anyone will hear and come.

He begins to get sleepy, hungry and cold,
a brave little boy, only eight years old.
Soon he sleeps, under the distant stars,
his peaceful mind dreams of men from Mars . . .

The trees exhale a sweet, sweet sound,
as delicate birds fly gently to the ground.
The boy awakens, the birds flutter away,
the nightmare is over as time brings along day.

Familiar voices are within a mile,
the boy widens his eyes and flashes a smile.

Karen Bethell

A War Zone

This gunfire has not ceased
And the amount of soldiers today have increased.
Over them border lines the enemies come forth in force
These ruthless men have no remorse,
Torture and death they endorse
And in our land all through this war
There is no law
Much bloodshed to be seen and upon the ground
Many corpses can be found
And also the stench of death lingers all around.
The nations have given much support
And all wonder when love and peace will be restored.
There is a solution yet amongst the world leaders such
A lot of confusion
And still there has been no resolution.

An invasion of army tanks moves slowly over those banks
And planes fly low ready to attack the target below.
Guns are loaded with ammunition
Then clasped in one hand all troops take up their position
And each man will make the last decision.
Bullets flew all around and in every direction
People run the battle had begun.
Unarmed and all these civilians are alarmed
And those merciless men brutally kill many of them.
Among the village these soldiers roam and pillage
The young and old live in fear
And when they are captured death draws near
The rest of the folk have fled
And in this place there is none to bury the dead.

Valerie Barton

WHIRLPOOL

I was a child innocent and happy playing in the sea,
Content with the world and had done no wrong.
Then anorexia came along and pulled me down,
Like a whirlpool - it was fast and vicious.

I tried to escape - but further down I went,
I stood alone - so no one saw,
Down I went - further, further with no escape.

Drowning in my despair the frustration grew,
My body had no chance to escape,
But I continued to fight - I wouldn't give in,

The whirlpool continued - round and round,
My feelings so strong and hard to beat,

Helpless, helpless, is how I felt,
The whirlpool in my life, was oh so harsh,
Evil, hatred it seemed to me,
But I knew that only I could set myself free.

I was tangled up, in so deep,
My energy was going, with little fight left,
Down, down my body went - until gone
Out of sight,

But then I saw a glimpse of light,
Was given some energy to help me fight,
And as I fought I slowly rose,

I was given strength, and I found the courage,
The whirlpool stopped and let me walk free,
I stood up tall and walked away from that evil,
Hatred sea.

Tracey Wheeler

EVERY POEM

Let me tell of my fiancée
My future wife to be,
Who lives not very far away
Just up the road from me.
She is loving, tender, caring
I know this to be true,
Before I tell you any more
Her Christian name is Sue.
She is very understanding
Her qualities they show,
The things I have been looking for
Which from her daily flow.
When I am in Sue's presence, then,
I have an inner peace,
For everything that is within
To her I do release.
I find it still so wonderful
To have a listening ear,
Thank God for 1998
An unexpected year!
He has given us each other
Our love we daily share,
The company, the fellowship,
The privilege of prayer.
Each other we do complement
In many different ways,
Since the Lord brought us together
Both hearts are full of praise.

Andrew Walker

WHEN TRIBAL MAN RETURNED

Once upon a time on earth
Came a hunter to find its worth.
Dark in heart, pale of face,
He multiplied a swirling race.
He travelled over land and sea
And saw a wealth all for free.

'Who are these species so pale of face?'
The tribal people felt unsafe.
So he fed them myths from his little black book
To multiply their fruitful looks.
But soon followed his colony
To end all the harmony.
This colossal impact changed all lives,
Spreading diseases, killing off tribes.
Rules were set and laws were laid,
Tribal man had no say.
He'd lost control of his vital land
And death resulted from making a stand.

There was nowhere where this hunter hadn't been.
Everywhere he made himself seen.
Disrupting, destroying, sustainable lives,
Disregarding traditional cries,
So ancient and wise.
For old tribal man swore to return
In a body so pale of face.
To teach him of the way of the land
Putting balance back into the place.
To destroy within, his ravaging brain
Before he swallowed up every grain,
And bring spirit and harmony back again.

Coleen O'Brien

The Ballad Of Fun

The stone flew high from the sling-shot strong,
It defeated the lamp with a shattering song.
Beneath the cover of the jet black of night,
The mischievous boys could do no right,
They reeked their vengeance with malice and anger,
When they left the street, the phone box stood no longer.

Now Micky was awoken in the dark of night,
By his mother and sister, screaming in fright.
He ran to his door and opened it wide,
But the heat and the smoke forced him back inside.
He picked up his chair, through the window it flew,
Then he shouted down, 'Hey you . . . hey you . . .
Our house is on fire, inside we are trapped . . .
Please call the brigade . . . there's a good chap!'

It was a full thirty minutes before they arrived.
Micky and his family had been burnt inside!
At the inquest, the coroner, he did ask,
'Now my good man, why did you not fulfil your task?'
'Your honour, I'm sorry,' the young man replied,
'But all the 'phone boxes had been vandalised!'

Helen Steel

HOMEWARD BOUND

The night was wild, a howling gale
Battered at the land so frail;
The waves were pounding on the shore
With promise of worse storms in store.
A few miles out and all alone
A trawler struggles to reach home;
Her nets in shreds, her tackle lost,
Her life itself, the final cost.
The aged frame that creaked and groaned,
The masts that swayed and softly moaned.
Little boat, you've done so well
To come home safely through this hell.
The rain beats down upon her deck
And waves reach up to claim the wreck.
The crew are tired, soaking, weak,
Attempt to plug up each new leak.
Their trust lies wholly in their craft
To hold together fore and aft.
Bravely, bravely, on she sped,
No one would give her up for dead!
And then at last, the lights of home
Are spied amidst the swirling foam.
The other boats tied to the pier,
That seem to say, 'We're glad you're here!'
Weary men climb onto land,
Each pulled up by a helping hand.
The little trawler sighs and moans;
Her masts still creak, her rigging groans.
She came home safe, the port was found -
Little trawler, safe and sound.

Jessica M A Thomas

MY LITTLE KITE

Some time ago when the winds died away,
a little kite decided to stay.
It gently drifted from above,
to show me friendship, peace and love.

It embraced me with colour and gaiety,
it made me laugh, be free and be me.

It opened a door to a place in my heart,
that up until then was tightly locked up.

This little kite became my friend,
devoted to him I was till the end.

I gave no thoughts to the winds in the sky,
the possibility that my little kite was just passing by.

Then one day so unexpectedly - the heavens called - to set my kite free.

No proper goodbyes we could say that day,
because none of us knew that my kite couldn't stay,

And the trees started stirring, a strong wind blew -
and away my little kite he flew.

And this is my story, though not the end,
because my little kite in my heart stays my friend,
and I look to the heavens, the winds and the tree,
and I know that my kite will be watching me.
And I know that in the winds he will reign,
until the day we will meet again.

R Widd

The Journey Home

As I walk all alone,
Fingers crossed to get home,
A drunk man laughs,
A baby cries,
The owls hoot,
The eerie sighs.

A cat jumps out to cause a fright,
Your eyes all over this haunted night,
Your heart beats quicker at every sound,
A creaking bush,
A howling hound.

As you reach your garden gate,
You walk in quiet because it's late,
When you're through you look behind,
Wondering what you might find.

You walk up to your front door,
Knowing that you're home once more,
Your panic's gone,
The night is still,
And like a glass,
Your heart can refill.

You're home at last,
Your problem's solved,
You feel content,
The night's evolved.

Barry Busby

THE NET

You thought you were safe, swimming in the sea.
Darting, and diving, you felt strong and free.
You did not see the net of swirling rope
Cast from a nearby fishing boat.
It came to rest so casually,
Like a coverlet, on top of the sea.
For a long, long time the net lay there.
And you underneath, were not aware
That the coverlet was beginning to sag
And turning into a huge round bag.
As fish could not escape the trap
You too were swept in through the gap.
There is no hope as you gasp for breath.
It is the end of life it is death.
Years, and years, and years, passed by
And now I know those fish did not die
For I have seen them swimming free
In a make-believe world but where is she?
Too small for her the glass-sided home
A miniature tropical sea kept warm
Sunlit by day and sunlit by night
No clouds ever to dim the light
There jewelled bodies glide as though through space
Between shells and ferns and rocks they race
But not to retreat or to hide, for they
Are cared for and protected from harmful prey
In a make-believe world but where is she?
She who was swept into the net by the sea.

M E C Houlden

BACK TO WORK

I woke up at dawn, but could I get back to sleep?
Thinking of what lay ahead, I felt that I could weep.
I tossed, I turned and went to the loo,
Sleep seemed to elude me, what was I going to do.
Try and think positive, I kept telling myself,
If you don't go back to work now, you'll be left on the shelf,
Unemployable, you've spent too much time at home,
I can imagine the scene, the employer talking in that tone.
No, it's best you go back now, the kids are now at school.
You can only do your best, but I just don't want to look a fool.
Eventually the alarm went off and with butterflies in my tum
In my smartest suit and make-up on, I decided it could be fun.
I then went into 'auto', got the kids up and fed,
Jumped into the car and off to work I sped.
The greeting at work was friendly and they had a sense of fun,
Inside I felt like eighteen, I had to remind myself I was a mum.
There seemed so much to take in, my brain seemed slow to get in gear,
But they didn't suspect, a calm exposure I kept, despite the fear.
Well soon the day was over, I couldn't wait to get home,
Picked the kids up from school and thought I'd use the phone.
How did my day go - well it went really well,
Described my day, the people, there was plenty I could tell.
Mum what's for tea, I'm hungry, then they started to have a row,
So I said goodbye and I realised the real work started now!

Yvonne Neal

STAND AND STARE

Will they care when I'm not there?
Maybe they will. Perhaps they will share
The many chores that fill my day
But no one is listening to what I say.
Breakfast odours fill the room
But what I see fills me with gloom
Table laden with many a dish
Not a crumb remains. Oh, how I wish
That I too could slam those doors
They don't look back. They hardly pause.
If only they knew how my heart does ache
To leave all behind and take a break
From busy day so full of duty
Mirror tells me I was quite a beauty.
My hair once black is now near white
My God, I look such an awful sight.
I see a brochure of azure seas
And painted houses, such sights to please.
Just let me go I beg of you
You'll get by; you'll all get through
And when I'm gone just maybe you'll care
That I've had no chance to stand and stare.
I'll return afresh to start once more
To tend your needs. I really do adore
Each one of you. You are my life
But see me more than just housewife
My mind is tired, my body taut
Give me a kindly second thought
When I return bright eyes will shine
As they did for Shirley Valentine.

Eileen St John-Crees

THE CHASUBLE OF SAINT ILDEFONSO

Once upon a time in Toledo, that rock and city of immortal fame,
There lived a holy bishop - Ildefonso was his name.
Though he was humble in heart, he was rich in faith and deeds.
He was a devoted pastor of his flock
Whom upon the sacraments and God's living Word he would feed.
And often would all Toledo flock to hear him preach -
For the way to eternal life to all the citizens he would teach.
Now, this Ildefonso was of Our Lady a most loyal friend,
Whose virginity and royal title,
Against the ravings of the renegades, he did valiantly defend.
And so, one day, in a dark Gothic chapel whilst he prayed,
The vault unfurled like a scroll - and the heavens were unveiled.
And lo - he beheld Our Lady in the royal rays of the sun enrobed,
Enthroned amidst the angels - her face as bright as snow.
And then, up, up leapt his soul - rapt like a dancing flame -
Transported by the cherubs to the throne of the glorious Dame,
Whereupon, woven by the angels, and not by human hand,
By her celestial majesty with a chasuble he was bestowed.
And thus, with wisdom garmented, and shining like a lamp,
For many years did this holy bishop govern and serve his fold
Until one day came when, like iron glowing in the forge,
Up rose his soul into the eternal light - to the bosom of the Lord.

John C Stratton

GREATER LOVE

    A call to be answered, a fight to be won,
A challenge thrown down to each mother's son.
    White feathers and shillings gleamed side by side
As they struggled with conscience and national pride;
    Yet prolific as words from the skilled writer's pen
Were the youth of the land who went forth like men.
    They went, yes they went, mere boys such as I,
Alone in their masses preparing to die.

    Bright bullets blackened in torn flesh and blood,
As the wounded lay helpless in rivers of mud.
    Sun baked their bodies, or rain-drenched their skin
As they thought of their homeland, determined to win
    Freedom from threat of tyrannical clutch
That clawed at their hearts with an icy touch;
    So they fought, yes they fought, mere boys such as I,
Alone in their trenches preparing to die.

    Spectral gauntlets haunted dark days,
Lashing crushed minds in the bloodiest affrays
    To the post of proud duty and blind charity,
Painting death visions with cruel clarity
    On fields of confusion, in which some would remain,
Lost to a world of long suffering and pain;
    For they went and they fought, for their comrades they cried;
Boys in their millions, alone as they died.

H Collister

OVERHEARD ON THE HIGHWAY

It looked so dejected standing there
Its leaf-laden boughs too tired to care
'Oh beech' said the silver birch, 'I feel so ill
My breathing is erratic and I'm shaking still
We used to breathe out oxygen to help the human race
But pollution's escalating and I can't keep up the pace.'
'Please don't give up dear silver birch for willow tree has news
Of a dedicated people who are called Friends of the Earth
They are protecting the environment and wisely know its worth
They're planting trees, recycling all products that are waste
Educating those who want to help 'going green' it must be faced
If planet Earth deserves survival there is much that must be done
Not only just a group but each and every one must play a vital part
If Earth is to survive or the people on this planet can never stay alive
Our roots go deep beneath the soil, for generations we've been here
So what chance have young saplings, it's pollution that I fear
All creatures on this planet great and small given by God alone
Could be a last existence unless priority's given protecting the ozone.'
'How come, silver birch you seem so well since you've got it
                                                                                        off your chest.'
'It's true dear beech it's the thought of those groups I've a feeling
They'll do their best. It's left to man to think and plan
While tree life takes a rest.'

Barbara Tunstall

GOLDFISH RECYCLING

When a friend of mine was twelve years old
She kept some fish which were coloured gold
They lived in a glass tank for all to see
We'd watch them all swimming quite happily.

On a weekly basis she'd clean out their tank
They'd be picked out so carefully in order of rank
She'd scrub all the gravel and rinse it all clean
It was the cleanest fish tank that I'd ever seen.

One day in the summer something just wasn't right
The fish changed their colour from golden to white
'Is there a heaven for goldfish?' she asked me that day
'I guess so' I answered, 'although who can say?'

She dug a small grave in the shade of the trees
Wrapped the fish in some velvet and knelt to her knees
She said her goodbyes to the fish which were dead
Laying down a few flowers and bowing her head.

An hour or so later while at a relative's farm
She played with the cat who lived in the barn
All of a sudden a thought crossed her mind
She had an idea, a spade she would find.

She went back to the garden and dug up the fish
She unrolled the velvet and got a small dish
The cat had a treat on that fine summer's day
And my friend helped recycling in her own little way.

Meinir

The Tramp

Take to the road, the life for me,
Just like the air and birds, I'm free
To wander at my will.
To climb with mountain sheep and goats
The highest peaks; and listen to the golden notes
That pour from a thousand golden throats,
Or the tinkle of a rill.

To sit beside the green hedgerow,
Where ragged robins wont to grow
And take my ease.
To watch the speckled butterfly
Dance in the sun; and chase the dappled meadow by,
Soft as a whisper, softly sigh,
What precious things are these.

But you can keep your smoky towns,
Give me the green and rolling Downs
Of Sussex and of Kent.
Give me the Yorkshire moors to roam
Just as I please; or, roofed by a verdant forest dome,
I'll rest awhile and make my home
In sweet content.

Cynthia C Berry

Natural Laws

You don't have to be talented, wise,
Or mature in advancing years to recognise,
That there are two laws of creative grace,
In the universality of this planetary place.

One is that things do seed and shoot
Upwards to a clearer space;
To spread out and absorb that above,
Producing in due season their gifted fruit.

The yield grows from air and light
As much as from root and soil;
For the benefit of all who stand
Wedded to their native land.

The other law Newton did so debate,
Is that a weighty thing returns to earth;
Like the apple in his garden one summer late
To the mother of its original birth.

These are scientific truths with creation bound,
And cannot be ignored or declared unsound;
Each is necessary for life and good,
Must be fully considered and understood.

Earthlings aspire to celestial thought,
Seek a vision beyond themselves;
But the ground pulls in a natural way,
Stopping all things falling apart.

Humankind can project for its gain
From the physical to the spiritual plane;
Though we reach for heaven outside,
The heaven within will also guide.

Eric Ashwell

STONES UPON THE WATER

I really love my brother
I hope that he loves me
when we feel that all is lost
we cast stones upon the sea.

The stones are flat and shiny
to skim across the water.
Some are small and tiny
others are much larger.

We skim them on the water
to see how far they go.
We watch them dance upon the ice
to see their happy glow.

We throw stones upon the water
to bond our male machismo.
The act itself symbolic
of our birth signs in Leo.

We do this for a while
aware of its deeper purpose.
Returning to our home once more
having grown closer, deep and morose.

We understand the stones' significance
as they bond us to each other
and leave the sandy shoreline
to welcome future brothers.

David C Love

Harry's Willow

Many years ago a twig was proffered by a friend
'Set it,' he said, 'and you will see a beautiful tree in the end'
It looked absolutely pathetic sat on the kitchen sill
In a bottle borrowed from the Co-op
I kept it warm until
Bottom roots assured me that life was there within
Harry was right - with a little help - the tree of life would begin

I've watched that tree throughout my life
As the seasons have come and gone
My willow was there when the babies were born
It's sympathetic when loved ones pass on
Time was when tree and I were slender
Today stout branches reach out afar
A lot has happened since I watched for roots
In the bottom of that glass jar

Sometimes, Harry's tree stands laughing
Reflecting the mood within our home
Not even the wind can contain happiness
As boughs sway and crisp leaves blow
Whenever I feel weepy the willow whistles me a tune
Cherub faces dodge the light
'Neath stars in a harvest moon
I can hear the children's laughter as they hide away from sight
Giggling midst piles of cushions in the land of pure delight
We all like to remember those long warm sunny days
Trees reflect life's pattern in so many different ways
There is no need to regret the things we think might have been
In life kindness grows to become tomorrow's dream
Harry gifted a twig - he had no reason to know
Just what influence he would have with that gesture long ago.

Frances Whitaker

THE CONFESSION

Father, I had to come today,
I've been at my wit's end the whole night,
I didn't mean to hit him that way,
And it's such a terrible sight.

Last night my Jim came home drunk again,
No wages for food or bills,
He'd been at the bookies with their Ben,
I think it was 'William Hills'.

Our little Joey had been playing football,
Earlier in the day,
And he broke her window - you know, Mrs Hall,
Who lives just across the way.

Well, someone had told Jim about it,
In the 'Bull's Head' on his way home,
So he stormed through the door in a real blue fit,
And our Joey was feared to the bone.

He took his belt off to get tough,
To strap the lad on the back,
But this time I thought enough is enough,
And I hit him with the vac.

Father, there wasn't too much blood,
I thought during the night he'd come round,
But he's still lying there like a lump of wood,
He hasn't made a sound.

Well, that's my confession Father dear,
What will they do to me?
Have I done the right thing in coming here,
Or should I have sent for the doctor maybe?

Jeanette Dykes

CHILD MISSING

'Child missing' the words spread
Swiftly, silently round.
Doors opened wide
Net curtains tweaked
A quiet sort of hubbub sound
From length to breadth of street.
With anxious eyes a-searching
And half-formed questions framed
On all the lips of neighbours
Can anyone be blamed?
Remembered clips from old newspapers
Invade the minds of those
Who cluster there and idly wait
For whispers heard at garden gate.
Mother just stands limply bemused
Dumb disbelief is on her face
Black fear within her heart,
Every second a minute becomes
Every minute an hour,
Till suddenly among the crowd
A whisper becomes a roar
'She's found, we've found her'
The people close their eyes
In quiet prayers of thankfulness
Some grip the mother's hand
Some look up to the skies
Replace the curtains, close the door,
The child is home once more.

Gwen Place

KING OF THE CUE

He is one ex-convict I was pleased to know
Who reshaped his life, as a sportsman-pro.

Fleeing from school early, he formed a gang
Of jobless laddies who stole, lazed and drank,
Drove powerful cars, and in pubs and bars
Displayed their deep-set drunk-brawl scars.

He was tried for every felony known to man
And, in a period of barely seven years' span
Was in and out of dark cells over a dozen times,
When his parents died - petrified by his crimes.

Daily he went to bed with a different street-girl,
He once said, his so-called machismo to unfurl,
And then was forced to seek refuge in a clinic -
Having with various viruses fallen sorely sick.

When he was twenty, yet behind prison walls
But in better health, an ex-champion of balls
Taught him to play skilled billiards and snooker,
And soon, at tables he unravelled dignified terror.

Taking advantage of most of their welfare schemes
In gaol, and by following all their rigorous regimes,
He earned early release for exceptional behaviour;
Then entered serious sport - helped by his saviour.

Now a millionaire, the world yields what is due
To this much-loved middle-aged King of the Cue.

Kopan Mahadeva

NORTHERN INTER-REALITY

The passenger sits transfixed,
Absorbing the light
Of passing reality
- From within the shade
Of scarlet seats,
While steel chants hypnotic
- From the cool depths below
And each posture is broken
By the surging beast,
Penetrating further
Into the motional dream.

The passenger whispers
A faint rebellion
And the beast responds
By testing its limits,
By swaying cross-purpose
Yet still confined
Like an animal caged
In the collective mind.

The passenger reclines.

'Out there lies something real
A view that we could steal,
Out there we'd free our minds
With the protean rhythm
Of pure perspective'.

Simon Dale Leeman

The Place

This is the place where the fishermen,
Go out to the waves and winds again,
Go out to the ebb and flow again,
And reap the wealth of the sea.

This is the place where the days are long,
And nights are filled, by a starry throng,
And the riding lights of ships belong
To the pulse in the ocean's heart.

This is the place where the tall cliffs span,
A sunny crescent of golden sand,
And brooding seaward, take their stand,
Against the deep waves' might.

This is the place where the seabirds cry,
Twilight and dawn, to a heedless sky.
But only the waves on the cliffs' reply,
'Your beauty passes, we endure.'

This is the place where the sunset burns,
On the waves' bright foam, when the slow tide turns,
And the heart and the soul together yearns,
For the peace and the hush of the deep.

W H Lunn

TALE OF THE CENTURY

As the century turned,
Queen Victoria died.
For sixty years,
she'd been our pride.

The Boer War over,
which relieved our men,
then in 1914,
to war again.

In roared the twenties,
they couldn't be stopped,
then Wall Street crashed,
and everything dropped.

In marched Hitler,
and Europe shook.
He pillaged and plundered,
he saw and he took.

The fifties arrived,
with slicked-back hair,
the young generation
made older folk stare.

The sixties swung,
the seventies rocked,
but in Vietnam,
the way was blocked.

The eighties and nineties,
the Falklands and Gulf,
will our New Century
be a lamb or a wolf!

David Price Edwards

Final Call

I am the modern mobile man
A city bred careerer
With one hand grip the wheel and steer
My four-by-four Frontera.

A belt and braces chap am I
And lethal at ten paces
When signals from my mobile fade
I park in empty places.

On blackened leaves the wipers brush
The inside fan is whirring
The office calls immediately
Before the engine's purring.

All meat to me are motorways
In blinding snow or raining
But I cut conversations short
To give the gal a caning.

The shares I see are up today
Each drop I am accustomed
So, on my calculator
Tap some figures to adjust them.

Ahead, the road is foggy calm
A distant light is flashing
If I pull out and . . .

Clive W Macdonald

WHEN FIRST WE MET

I searched the endless sea of faces in the room that night
I gazed across the smoke-filled room into the semi-light.
And as I gazed so aimlessly, wondering what to do
What happened next, I can't explain - because I was looking at you!

How could it be that just one look, just one little touch
Could bring us both together - and make me feel so much?
The past was all forgotten and the future beckoned me,
And when you gazed into my eyes - that's all that I could see.

How long we gazed I could not tell, my soul was torn asunder
And from the depths of my whole being, I felt a thrill of wonder.
From that moment my whole past was hidden from my view,
Being with you in the present was all I ever knew.

My mirthful laughter bubbled up, my cares were swept aside,
I knew no weariness at all, just warm content inside.
The room was filled with laughter and the band was playing too
But what was playing I could not tell - I neither cared nor knew.

Then somehow we were quite alone, your friends had moved away,
What could I do, what could I think, whatever could I say?
As slowly and with gentleness you put me at my ease,
The bitter cold made me tremble - I thought that I would freeze.

But strangely it was not the cold that made me shiver so,
For when you looked into my eyes, my heart warmed with a glow,
Strange chaos stirred my very soul, the ground around me rocked,
I gazed in wonderment at you - and all we did was talk!

I tasted the wine you gave me, I drank it deep and long,
My heart was a flame of fire and my soul was alive with song.
And on that night I realised I loved you for all time,
No will, no purpose of my own, this surely was no crime?

Hazel Barber

A Long-Lost Moment

From that 'Atlantis' continent
He phoned me.
I did not talk then
I did not notice,
The season failed to wake
A slave - called housewife.
Some cook books
A family to feed
I got old at twenty-three.

After thirty years
A tiny news found me.
He waited
Once in spring.
All day long - alone
Composing a song
Under a greenest flowery tree.

Thirty years gone
The tree has turned to wood.
A woman in a tailored society
Is now really old.

Saleha Chowdhury

SUBMISSIONS INVITED
SOMETHING FOR EVERYONE

POETRY NOW '99 - Any subject, any style, any time.

WOMENSWORDS '99 - Strictly women, have your say the female way!

STRONGWORDS '99 - Warning! Age restriction, must be between 16-24, opinionated and have strong views. (Not for the faint-hearted)

All poems no longer than 30 lines.
Always welcome! No fee!
Cash Prizes to be won!

Mark your envelope (eg *Poetry Now*) '99
Send to:
Forward Press Ltd
1-2 Wainman Road, Woodston,
Peterborough, PE2 7BU

OVER £10,000 POETRY PRIZES TO BE WON!

Judging will take place in October 1999